THE APPLE
EXPERIENCE

THE APPLE EXPERIENCE

SECRETS
TO BUILDING
INSANELY GREAT
CUSTOMER
LOYALTY

CARMINE GALLO

Mc
Graw
Hill

NEW YORK   CHICAGO   SAN FRANCISCO
LISBON   LONDON   MADRID   MEXICO CITY   MILAN
NEW DELHI   SAN JUAN   SEOUL   SINGAPORE
SYDNEY   TORONTO

Copyright ©2012 by Carmine Gallo. All rights reserved. Manufactured in the United States of America. Except as permitted under the United States Copyright Act of 1976, no part of this publication may be reproduced or distributed in any form or by any means, or stored in a data base or retrieval system, without the prior written permission of the publisher.

Library of Congress Cataloging-in-Publication Data

Gallo, Carmine.
    The Apple experience : the secrets of delivering insanely great customer service / by Carmine Gallo. — 1st ed.
        p. cm.
    ISBN-13: 978-0-07-179320-9 (alk. paper)
    ISBN-10: 0-07-179320-8 (alk. paper)
    1. Customer services.   2. Consumer satisfaction.   3. Creative thinking.   I. Title.
    HF5415.5.G356 2012
    658.8'12—dc23

                                                                        2012005418

1 2 3 4 5 6 7 8 9 0 DOC/DOC 1 8 7 6 5 4 2

ISBN 978-0-07-179320-9
MHID   0-07-179320-8

e-book ISBN 978-0-07179321-6
e-book MHID   0-07179321-6

McGraw-Hill books are available at special quantity discounts to use as premiums and sales promotions, or for use in corporate training programs. To contact a representative please e-mail us at bulksales@mcgraw-hill.com.

The Apple Experience is in no way authorized, prepared, approved, or endorsed by Apple Inc.

This book is printed on acid-free paper.

To Vanessa, Josephine, and Lela

Contents

Acknowledgments

The Apple Experience is a collaboration of colleagues, friends, editors, and readers around the world who have requested new content that helps them understand and apply the magic behind the Apple adventure.

It's been a gratifying experience to work with McGraw-Hill Professional. Thanks to everyone at the company in editing, sales, marketing, public relations, and digital who are strong advocates of the book. Special thanks to Philip Ruppel, Mary Glenn, Ann Pryor, and Ruth Mannino for your guidance. I'd also like to offer a shout-out to my former editor, Gary Krebs, who shared the vision for a book that could lift the veil behind Apple's award-winning customer culture.

Roger Williams takes special care to consider the long-term interests and careers of his clients. It's an honor to call him my agent and friend.

Tom Neilssen and Les Tuerk at BrightSight Group are extraordinary speaking agents who successfully help me share my ideas with audiences around the world. I'm grateful for their partnership.

Publicity is a collaborative effort, and an author couldn't have it better than to count on Mark Fortier and his team at Fortier Public Relations.

This book owes its accomplishment to my colleagues at Gallo Communications who dedicated hours of research and valuable insights: Carolyn Kilmer, Sarah Daniels, Tamara Medina, and Vanessa Gallo. Vanessa worked tirelessly to help organize ideas, edit, and format. Her background in psychology and customer service also proved to be invaluable.

Although my family is last in the acknowledgments, they come first in my life. They're everything to me and bring me more joy each day. My wife, Vanessa, and girls, Josephine and Lela, are the light of my life. My mother, Giuseppina, and my in-laws, Ken and Patty, all deserve my gratitude, as do Tino, Donna, Francesco, and Nick. Finally, none of my success would be possible if hadn't been for my late father, Francesco Gallo, who had the courage to seek a better life for his family. We owe him everything.

Enriching Lives

*We are at our best when we deliver
enriching experiences.*

—Apple credo

G ary Allen traveled 3,200 miles, crossed ten states, and used 100 gallons of gas to celebrate the tenth anniversary of the Apple Store in May 2011. Why would he do such a thing?

When the iPad was introduced, thousands of people camped out overnight at Apple Stores around the world to be among the first customers to buy it. Even Apple cofounder Steve Wozniak stood in line at a store in San Jose, California, more than *twelve hours* before the device went on sale! Couldn't he have simply called his boyhood pal, Steve Jobs, and ask for an iPad to be delivered to his home?

Comedian Mark Malkoff brought a goat into an Apple Store—yes, a real goat—posted the video on YouTube and received nearly one million views.[1] He also decided to test the patience of Apple employees by ordering pizza and having it delivered to him at an Apple location, visiting stores dressed as Darth Vader, and hiring a trumpet player to serenade him and his wife *in an actual store*. Why didn't Apple Store managers kick him out? The answers to these questions will help you create a one-of-a-kind experience for your customers that will move your brand forward and help you crush your competitors. But to really understand the answers, we have to turn to a higher source.

Gimme That Ol' Time Apple Religion

One of the most intense religious experiences of my life happened when I was a graduate student of journalism at Northwestern University. One Sunday a group of us decided to attend a Baptist church in downtown Chicago. Keep in mind that as a Catholic boy from California this was my first "immersive" experience outside of a Catholic mass. You could imagine how puzzled I must have been to see nurses standing alongside the walls. Once women started fanning themselves and fainting during the service, I knew why the nurses had been stationed there! When I saw the twenty-member gospel choir starting to rock out to the song "I'm Going with Jesus" and the preacher running full speed around the perimeter of the church with his arms in the air, I realized this would be unlike anything I ever experienced at my church. Those churchgoers were truly "inspired"—infused with the spirit.

Many Apple customers are also infused with the spirit—the Apple spirit. In 2011 researchers in the United Kingdom discovered that Apple actually triggers the same areas of the brain that light up during intensely religious experiences. The neuroscientists used magnetic resonance imaging (MRI) technology to discover that, for Apple fans, seeing images of Apple products actually lit up the same parts of the brain as images of a deity do for religious people. If you've seen photos or videos of customers whipped up in a sort of "evangelical frenzy" at Apple Store openings, now you understand why.

Oakland, California, resident Gary Allen is one of the faithful. In May 2011, Allen marked the tenth anniversary of the Apple Store by traveling thousands of miles to visit the first store in Tysons Corner, Virginia. He didn't even fly. He rented a Toyota Yaris and drove for five days. Allen began his trip on Saturday, May 14, headed along I-80 to Denver and through Kansas, Missouri, Pennsylvania, and into Virginia. Now get this. Allen didn't even know how

Apple would celebrate the anniversary. He just knew how *he* would celebrate—by making a pilgrimage to the place where it all began.

After Allen's final long night of driving and getting just four hours of sleep, Allen arrived on the sixth day of his journey at 9:40 a.m. No special event had been scheduled. No reporters were present, and no banners unfurled. But since Allen had been blogging about his journey, the Apple employees knew about his arrival, gave him a tour of the store, and even treated him to cake. Allen was filled with the Apple spirit. For Allen, visiting an Apple Store is a religious experience. Religion gives meaning to people's lives, and for millions of Apple customers and thousands of employees, the brand gives them a sense of meaning, providing deeply emotional experiences that improve their lives.

A Puddle of Water Turns to a Pile of Panic

One early morning I awoke to find a puddle of water at the base of our refrigerator. It had stopped working overnight, and the freezer's ice had completely melted, not to mention the ice cream and other products. In my attempt to be a good husband, I decided to troubleshoot before my wife and kids woke up. I called the Sears customer service number placed on the inside of the unit, peaceful in the knowledge that all would be well soon.

The Sears phone tree took me through a menu of options, but I was still relatively calm until an automated voice informed me that the next available day for repair would be "Thursday," a full week from the time I was calling. A small panic began to set in. Finally I reached a live human being, and my panic began to subside until he put me on hold...and that's when my peace was shattered for good. My wife walked in as I was on hold and asked who I was on the phone with.

"I'm on hold with Sears customer service. Our refrigerator is broken." I said. My wife glared at me and through gritted teeth said, "I vowed never to do business with Sears again."

She reminded me that she had a troubling in-store customer experience at a local Sears store the previous year followed by endless red tape and frustration. I recalled the incident but thought it was a fluke, and besides, customer service on the phone must be a completely different experience.

Since I was in the middle of researching this book, I decided to turn a potential negative into a positive and conduct some research. While I was on hold for a considerable amount of time, I conducted a Twitter search for the term "Sears customer service." I wish I hadn't. Here is just a sample of the remarks left by Sears customers within a twenty-four-hour period:

- "Sears is the worst. There's a dozen customer service counters, and no one at them."

- "I haven't bought from @sears in over 30 years. Their service ALWAYS sucks."

- "Sears home service and customer solutions should be ashamed and shut down."

- "Sears customer solutions is rude and has no solutions."

- "Parents about to lose it with Sears customer service count 5... 4...3...2..."

- "Sears, I'm done with you. Your customer service is deplorable & I will never EVER buy another product from your stores again."

Just then a customer service rep returned to the phone. I was hesitant to proceed but didn't know what else to do. The milk was getting warm, the ice was melting, and my kids would be up any minute. So I forged ahead.

"We can send a repair technician to your house today if you purchase the $250 extended care agreement," the phone rep said curtly. He also explained that it would take care of all parts and labor. I knew I was being manipulated into purchasing something I didn't need, but if it would guarantee a repairman to my house "today" instead of next week, I would do it. After giving my credit card information to the rep, he informed me that it would include all parts and labor only "up to $500." Again, I felt manipulated. The peace, which had turned to panic, had now turned to aggravation. To cap it off, the phone rep repeatedly stated in question format, "OK? OK?" to get me off the phone. I got off the phone feeling angry, frustrated, and manipulated, and just a few minutes earlier I had awoken as a very happy man, looking forward to another great day.

On a whim, I decided to see what Apple customers were feeling that day. Here's a sample of Twitter remarks from the same twenty-four-hour per period as my Sears search:

- "Though I'm generally a skeptical customer, I truly couldn't be more pleased w/the service I received at our local mall's Apple store. #happy."

- "Apple has always amazed me with their awesome customer service. #1 IMO!"

- "It's really hard to knock the Apple Store employees because the customer service is awesome. But c'mon, too hipster."

- "Thanks to Apple for replacing my dead iPhone with very little fuss. Great customer service."

- "I must say Apple Store has supreme customer service."

- "Apple has the best customer service in the history of service."

- "Apple has just made me the happiest person in the world. Great customer service!"

Three months after my experience with Sears, the company dropped a bombshell, announcing that it would close 120 stores and lay off thousands of people after a significant drop in same-store sales. Sears blamed the economy, but retail experts pointed to a severe decline in customer service as the primary culprit behind Sears's trouble.

What was the difference? How does Apple succeed when so many others fail? What is Apple doing right? Most important, what principles can any business learn from Apple about creating an extraordinary customer experience? It starts by asking the right questions. While Sears leaders were asking themselves, "Where are the best places to cut expenses?" Apple senior executives including

Steve Jobs were asking, "Who provides the world's best customer service?"

Stuff You Don't Learn in School

I hold a unique position within the Apple community. My book *The Presentation Secrets of Steve Jobs* is an international bestseller and has changed the way entrepreneurs and business leaders around the world tell their brand stories. In some countries such as Japan, it has become one of the most successful nonfiction books in recent history. Everyone, it seems, wants to communicate better, and who better to learn from than the late Steve Jobs, the master of communication? The principles outlined in the book are catching on. When Facebook founder Mark Zuckerberg introduced a redesign to the site, many observers on Twitter suggested that he must have read the book since he was dissecting a Steve Jobs presentation scene for scene. It's all very flattering, but nothing replaces the joy I get when I receive e-mails from people who have used the principles to successfully attract investors, win multimillion-dollar contracts, pitch movie scripts, or simply to get an A on their school presentations.

I followed the presentation book with another bestseller, *The Innovation Secrets of Steve Jobs*. This book, too, changed the way businesses around the world think about their products, customers, and communication. I've presented the content to audiences around the world as well as MBA classes at Stanford, Berkeley, and UCLA among others. On every campus I get the same reaction. Students will approach me and say, "We never learn this stuff in school."

My books have won many fans within Apple itself. Some Apple Store managers have told me that they require new employees to read my books before their first training session. I've even met Apple Store employees who say they were asked to read *The Presentation Secrets of Steve Jobs* so they could apply some of the communications techniques to the experience on the sales floor. It soon became obvious that another book was required to round out the trilogy and help readers understand what it means to deliver an Apple-like experience in any industry.

Whenever I visit an Apple Store and I meet people who have read my book, I ask them questions—lots and lots of questions. Why did you greet me at the door? Why do you wear a blue shirt? Why do you use two fingers to point somewhere? Why do you use my first name several times in the conversation? Why did you spend twenty minutes talking football instead of selling me a product? Why do you want me to be the first to touch a product? Some people must think I'm a nut, but there's a method behind the madness. I'm a journalist, I love to solve communication challenges, and I really enjoy breaking them down into a simple approach that anyone can follow. I'm constantly asking myself, *Why does Apple do what it does, what other brands do something similar, and how can I teach these principles to others?*

I don't bill myself as a "customer service expert." I'm a communications coach, speaker, and journalist. But what does it mean to provide extraordinary customer service? Well, if you study the brands that do it well such as Disney, Four Seasons, Zappos, FedEx, Nordstrom, Apple, and others, you will discover that it all comes down to communication: how you talk to your employees and how they, in turn, talk to your customers. In fact, Apple did not invent many of its customer service principles. Steve Jobs has acknowledged that the Apple Store was inspired by the Four Seasons (which is why the hotel chain and other brands are discussed in this book). But Apple has refined and improved upon the principles it learned from others. Apple has, in turn, inspired many brands that touch your life. AT&T made changes in its retail store experience with input from Steve Jobs himself. Disney, Nike, T-Mobile, Tesla, J.C. Penney, and other brands have done the same. You can, too.

The principles in this book work for Apple, and they'll work for you, too. I'll show you the parallels, but it's up to you to adopt the techniques. Each chapter reviews one principle. At the end of each chapter, "check out" the activities that will force you to think differently about the experience you provide and how to apply the techniques in the chapter. You will also see real customer reaction quotes throughout the chapters. If you are not hearing the same enthusiastic feedback from your customers, then you need to dedicate yourself to implementing the tactics discussed in the chapter.

The Apple Experience Made Simple

The Apple Experience is divided into three parts. Part I, "Inspiring Your Internal Customer," focuses on employees, training, and internal communications. Part II, "Serving Your External Customer," reveals specific techniques to wow your customers in every conversation. Part III, "Setting the Stage," discusses the environment in which you present yourself, your brand, and your product. Although each of the parts is equally important to providing an Apple experience, most observers stick to what they can see—Apple products and the design of the stores. The Apple experience is so much more. "If Apple products were the key to the Stores' success, how do you explain the fact that people flock to the stores to buy Apple products at full price when Walmart, Best-Buy, and Target carry most of them, often discounted in various ways, and Amazon carries them all—and doesn't charge sales tax!"[2] according to Apple's former head of retail, Ron Johnson. "People come to the Apple Store for the experience—and they're willing to pay a premium for that."

Enriching Lives

All Apple employees are encouraged to carry a credo card, a wallet-sized card that outlines the vision behind the Apple Retail Store. The first two words on the front of the card are "Enriching Lives." Those are the two most important words in this book. According to Ron Johnson, retailers should be asking themselves, "How do we reinvent the store to enrich our customers' lives?"[3] When you enrich the lives of your employees, they are more engaged in your business, are less likely to leave, and offer better customer service. When you enrich the lives of your customers or clients, they will reward you with their business and, more important, become your most ardent fans and actively promote your business to others. When you enter the business of "enriching lives," magical things start to happen. Let's make magic together.

INSPIRING YOUR INTERNAL CUSTOMER

*The most important component
to the Apple experience is that the
staff isn't focused on selling stuff. It's
focused on building relationships and
trying to make people's lives better.*
—Ron Johnson

When the Apple Store celebrated its tenth anniversary, the majority of media articles credited its success to products and design, but as Ron Johnson has pointed out, those are only a small piece of the experience puzzle. If your employees are not trained, personable, and passionate about the brand, you'll have no chance of building a company that delivers an Apple quality experience.

Sadly, many companies rank low on the customer satisfaction index because their employees are discouraged, disillusioned, and uninspired. Gallup has found that 71 percent of employees in the United States are "not engaged" or worse, "actively disengaged and emotionally disconnected" from their workplaces.[1] This is a shocking observation. Seventy percent of employees are emotionally disconnected. That means they simply don't care about their job and their company. No wonder customer service is the pits. Offering more perks like free soda in the vending machine or free-pizza Friday won't change the culture. People want to be inspired. They want to work toward a higher purpose and to feel good about themselves and the brands they work for.

I once met a college student, Lynda, whose former boyfriend was a changed man after only two months at the Apple Store. She told me that if he had exhibited the same traits when they were dating, the two would still be together!

"What was different about him?" I asked Lynda. She said, "He was more confident. He could talk to people easier. He was less judgmental. He was a better listener. It sounds cliché, but he was the guy who I knew he was capable of becoming!"

Apple touches the lives of its customers only after touching its employees. "Why do you like working here?" I once asked an enthusiastic Apple employee. "Even people who walk in here upset leave happy," he said. "It's a rewarding experience, improving people's lives for the better. That's pretty special." It sure is, and that's why we need to study and emulate the experience.

CHAPTER 1

Dream Bigger

We attract a different type of person,
someone who really wants to get in a
little over his head and make a dent
in the universe.

—Steve Jobs

A s the world mourned the passing of Steve Jobs in October 2011, commentators were discussing the principles that made Apple a success. During an interview with the ABC News program *20/20*, correspondent Deborah Roberts asked me about the role vision played in Steve Jobs's success. "Vision is everything," I said. "A bold dream attracts evangelists, and no lasting brand can be built without a team of dedicated people who share the vision. Passion fuels the rocket; vision directs the rocket to its ultimate destination." You simply cannot build an organization that delivers an extraordinary customer experience unless you have a clear vision of the type of experience you plan to offer.

How did Steve Jobs start a company in the garage of his parents' house and grow it into one of the most valuable companies on the planet? Did it take passion? You bet. Hard work? Creativity? Ingenuity? Yes, yes, and yes. But it all started with a vision that could not be contained within the small confines of the garage: to put a computer in the hands of everyday people. Once the vision was established, everything else fell into place. Vision was everything. Steve Jobs's vision was not to make a load of money and retire on a yacht. (In fact with the exception of a corporate jet, Jobs lived a humble lifestyle. Microsoft cofounder Bill Gates once visited Jobs at his home and wondered how so many people could fit in such a modest dwelling.) Jobs's vision was to make tools that would help people unleash their personal creativity. He wanted to build a company that would outlast him. He wanted to build a legacy. "Being the richest man in the cemetery doesn't matter to me," Steve Jobs once said. "Going to bed at night saying, 'We've done something wonderful,' that's what matters to me."

A vision helps you see things that others might have missed. For example, when Steve Jobs and Steve Wozniak started Apple on April 1, 1976, "Woz" shared Jobs's vision to build "personal" computers that average people could use and enjoy. The Apple II became the most popular personal computer of its time, but it was still not ready to enter the homes of everyday people. In 1979 Jobs was given a tour of the Xerox research facility in Palo Alto, California. There, for the first time, he saw a crude "graphical user interface" where a user would interact with a computer via colorful icons on the screen and a gadget called a "mouse." Jobs instantly saw the potential of the technology for satisfying his vision of bringing a computer into the homes of everyday people. Jobs once said Xerox could have dominated the entire computer industry but did not because the Xerox vision was limited to building another copy machine. In other words, two people can see the same thing but interpret it differently based on their vision.

The Real Beginning of the Apple Store

Steve Jobs had a lot in common with country music superstar Garth Brooks. Both artists were inspired by innovators who paved the road ahead of them. I saw Brooks perform a one-man show at the Wynn hotel in Las Vegas in which he captivated the audience for more than two hours. When Brooks walked on stage, he told the audience that for them to really understand his music, he would have to start from the beginning. Brooks explained that his musical career did not begin with his first single. Instead his inspiration started in the 1960s, when his parents would bring home new albums in both country and contemporary styles. If Brooks had played only his hits during the Wynn performance, it would have been a richly satisfying experience for Garth fans. But by taking his audience on a journey through the music that inspired him, Brooks created an unmatched and memorable experience for everyone in his audience, country and noncountry fans alike. So let's steal a page from the Garth Brooks songbook and start from the real beginning of the Apple experience.

> *If every retail store had customer service like Apple, the world would be a better place.* —Michael M.

The One Question That Unleashed Apple's Success

When the Apple Store celebrated its ten-year anniversary on May 19, 2011, the media focused on the growth story: one billion visitors, 325 stores, $10 billion in sales, and so on. The numbers were and continue to be astonishing: $6 billion in quarterly revenue, $4,700 in sales per square foot, and 22,000 weekly visitors in a typical store. But numbers alone won't teach you anything. It's the story behind the numbers where you'll learn how to turn your business into an experience so thrilling that your customers will become true advocates for your brand.

The story of the Apple experience did not begin with the opening of the first Apple Store at Tysons Corner, Virginia, in 2001. It began forty years earlier with the founding of another brand that would be credited with completely reinventing the customer experience—the Four Seasons. When Steve Jobs first decided to enter the retail business, he hired former Target executive Ron Johnson. Jobs challenged Johnson with this question: who offers the best customer service experience in the world? The answer was not another computer retailer—or any retailer for that matter. The answer turned out to be the Four Seasons hotel. Just as Garth Brooks did not invent country music, Steve Jobs did not invent exceptional customer service. Both artists, however, copied a great idea, refined it, and took it to the next level.

The Brand That Inspired Apple Retail

Isadore Sharp founded the Four Seasons in 1960, but it took another decade for the brand to become synonymous with luxury. Prior to building his first luxury hotel in London in 1970, Sharp's experience had been limited to building homes, apartments, and small motels in Toronto. But homes were too small for Sharp's outsized ambition. Sharp's goal—his vision—was to create a worldwide luxury brand that would offer an unparalleled customer experience. Most bold visions are met with a high degree of skepticism, and Sharp's vision was no exception. Sharp's wife, Rosalie, admits that she didn't share Sharp's confidence, but thankfully for the Fours Seasons, Rosalie kept her reservations to herself.

Like Steve Jobs, Sharp was a dreamer. He refused to settle for anything less than excellence. "So much of long-term success is based on intangibles. Beliefs and ideas. Invisible concepts,"[1] Sharp once said. Once Sharp's vision was set—a worldwide brand of luxury hotels that offer exceptional customer service—he had to fill in the blanks. Sharp asked, "What would that luxury experience look and feel like?" You might be surprised to learn that the innovations that follow are all thanks to Sharp and the Four Seasons:

- **Travel-Size Shampoo.** Having grown up with three sisters, Sharp learned a few things about women and their travel habits. He learned that they didn't like to wash their hair with soap, so they carried small bottles of shampoo. The Four Seasons was the first hotel to put shampoo bottles in every room. Would you expect anything less today, even from the lowest budget chain?

- **Fitness Rooms.** Sharp liked to exercise, and he knew that travelers would need a revival, especially after long flights. The Four

Seasons was the first hotel to provide fitness centers. The next time you jump on the treadmill at your hotel, you've got Sharp to thank.

- **Comfortable Beds.** Sharp's first hotel in London catered to American travelers, many of whom would fly overnight from the East Coast. Above all else, those weary customers wanted a comfortable bed. Sharp searched several countries in Europe before he found a bed that met his standard for comfort. The Four Seasons offered the most comfortable beds of any hotel chain at the time, and today there seems to be an all-out war among hotels to see who has the best beds.

- **Full-Service Spas.** In 1986 a Four Seasons resort north of Dallas was the first to introduce a full-service spa on the property. Anytime you get a relaxing massage on your hotel's property, you can credit Sharp's vision. He knew what travelers wanted even before they could express it themselves, just as Jobs knew what Apple consumers would want before they knew it themselves.

Sharp was responsible for many, many more innovations. "We initiated many ideas to enhance customer appreciation,"[2] said Sharp. "We introduced no-smoking floors. We anticipated trends in low-fat, low-salt haute cuisine. We put shampoo, hair dryers, makeup mirrors, and bathrobes in rooms for guests who prefer to travel light. Each room was slightly larger than our competitors' regular rooms, with quieter plumbing, a better showerhead, and a bed with a comfortable, custom-made mattress."

The Four Seasons, in turn, inspired some of Apple's retail innovations. Steve Jobs and Ron Johnson asked themselves, "What would the Four Seasons do?" For starters, the Four Seasons does not have cashiers. Instead it has a concierge (another innovation that Sharp brought from Europe to the U.S. hotel industry). When the Apple stores first opened, a "concierge" greeted customers. Although the concierge title no longer exists, a greeter still stands at the door ready to welcome customers into the store. Apple copied another Four Seasons innovation: the bar. Walk into an Apple Store and you'll find a bar, just like the Four Seasons. There is one difference: The Four Seasons bar dispenses alcohol. The Apple Genius Bar dispenses advice.

The Genius Bar is an example of connecting ideas from different fields, a concept I explore in *The Innovation Secrets of Steve Jobs.* Your customer experience is only going to be as good as the model you use for inspiration. Studying brands outside of your industry can spark creative brainstorms. Johnson was actually the first person to come up with the idea of the Genius Bar after listening to members of his retail development team. According to Jobs's biographer, Walter Isaacson, Jobs thought it was a crazy idea. But Johnson was a fearless employee (a concept you'll learn in Part I) and stood his ground. The next day Jobs had filed to trademark the name, Genius Bar.

The Three-Word Vision That Built FedEx

Michael Basch learned the power of vision at FedEx. During his ten years as senior vice president of sales and customer service, he helped take FedEx from $0 to over $1 billion. Today everyone knows FedEx's three-word vision: Absolutely, Positively, Overnight. After its first day in operation, however, FedEx managers communicated a different three-word vision to their employees: *get the packages.*

Basch, Fred Smith, and the other senior executives at FedEx were justifiably anxious on the new carrier's first day of operation on March 12, 1973. After years of planning, FedEx had twenty-three airplanes positioned in ten cities. Dozens of salespeople were ready to accommodate the flood of orders. There was one thing they didn't expect—no packages. On the first day of operation, FedEx delivered exactly *two packages*! Founder Fred Smith had the great idea of creating a customer-focused delivery system based on the motto, "People-Service-Profit." But the company would be out of business within a week if it didn't get the packages.

FedEx managers made the decision to communicate that vision—get the packages—and get out of the way of employees who were tasked with accomplishing the vision. In his book, *Cus-*

tomer Culture, Basch tells the story of Diane, a tracking clerk, who received a call from a distraught bride-to-be who needed a wedding dress to be delivered for her big day, which happened to be *the next day*. The dress, however, was 300 miles away. Diane had internalized the vision and did what had to be done. She lined up a Cessna and a pilot to fly the package to Florida. The bride was so ecstatic she called Diane from her honeymoon! She said the FedEx story stole the show. Everyone at the wedding was talking about the company that gave a wedding dress its own plane.

When Diane told Basch about the situation, he was taken aback. They would surely go bankrupt if they kept pulling these stunts, he thought. But Diane could not be faulted for creatively executing on the vision. It didn't take long for Basch to come around. One company executive who heard the wedding story assigned his company's shipments to FedEx and began sending twenty packages via the service. Others at the wedding began using FedEx as their exclusive priority delivery company and continued to do so for years. According to Basch, "The biggest lesson was that if you were clear about what you wanted as leaders and then let people give it to you without tying their hands behind their backs, you got it."[3]

In hindsight, Basch believes it would have been worse if FedEx had delivered 300 packages on its first day. Why? Early success breeds complacency. FedEx might have become sloppy about service and the customer experience. Instead, everyone began to obsess about creating an extraordinary service culture. According to Basch, "One of the most valuable lessons was the power of people when they have a common vision and commitment."[4]

Basch says that a well-designed culture has six primary attributes, the first of which is vision, a clear picture of the desired customer experience (the other five are also relevant to the Apple experience and will be explored in the next chapters). "The vision provides the light and the gravitational force. The vision is the compass of the enterprise—its purpose for being. More practically and specifically, it is the experience that the organization is attempting to create for its customers, employees, and owners . . . the experience is then condensed into a headline that provides direction."[5]

The Apple Vision: Enriching Lives

Let's get back to the vision behind the Apple Store. Recall from my introduction, the vision behind Apple Retail can be found on the credo card: Enriching Lives. The former head of Apple Retail, Ron Johnson, said that when Apple opened its first retail store, not one analyst gave Apple a chance. Apple had 3 percent market share, Gateway had shuttered its retail because the stores were attracting only 200 or so people a week (today 22,000 people a week visit the typical Apple Store), and Apple was competing against computer players like Dell whose slim margins and lower costs seemed to be the preferred business model.

According to Johnson, "A vision is something that you can say in one sentence. The fewer words the better. It's like saying 'A thousand songs in your pocket.' It's a clear vision that everyone understands."[6] Johnson and Jobs decided to craft visions for their competitors. For example, retailers like Gateway "sell boxes." Johnson believes a company vision will lead it to pursue a very specific set of conclusions about the experience it offers. So if your vision is to sell boxes or "stack 'em high and let 'em fly," as some retailers do, it will lead to a business model that competes on price and price alone. For some large retailers, offering the cheapest price on the block has clearly been a formula for success. But most businesses cannot simply compete on price. They must differentiate on the customer experience. "When we envisioned the Apple model, we said that it has got to connect with Apple," said Johnson. "So it was easy. Enriching lives. That's what Apple had been doing for thirty years."

When a company starts with a vision such as "enriching lives," magical things begin to happen. For Apple, "enriching lives" meant offering one-to-one training and group workshops for people who wanted to release their inner Scorsese, directing and editing their own movies, publishing their family memories, or dreaming of becoming rock stars. Steve Jobs said that people didn't want to buy computers; they wanted to know what they could do with those computers. Jobs understood that his customers didn't want to walk out of a store with a box. They wanted to leave with a tool to help them fulfill their dreams.

After dealing with Apple, you feel it's not like Apple has the best customer service, but Apple is the only company that has customer service. —Rohit A.

The Devil's in the Details, but Success Comes from Above

Steve Jobs was fanatical about the details of the customer experience. Jobs once called an executive who worked for an Apple partner and asked, "Are you mad at your customers?" The executive had spoken to Jobs before, so he wasn't surprised that Jobs had called. He was taken aback by the question, however. "We're not mad at our customers at all," he replied. "Then why does your disclosure statement sound so angry?" Steve Jobs asked. "You should be more friendly to your customers at every touchpoint."

Steve Jobs had reviewed every line of the "terms and conditions" agreement that most customers check or sign, but never read. It mattered to him. The screens of notebook computers in Apple stores are positioned at ninety-degree angles to force customers to reposition the screen to interact with the product. Positions matter. Apple employees wear blue shirts to stand out in crowded stores. Colors matter. Customers are greeted within ten seconds and ten feet of walking through the door. Greetings matter. Nothing about the customer experience is taken for granted. Not one thing. Details mean everything in the Apple experience, and Apple studies everything about the customer interaction to learn, refine, and improve. But while the "devil's in the details," an innovative customer experience cannot happen in the absence of a loftier goal, an inspiring vision that attracts evangelists and reveals every ounce of your creativity and potential. Steve Jobs and Ron Johnson had a vision—to enrich lives. What's yours?

CHECKOUT

1. **Find inspiration outside your industry.** Steve Jobs once said, "Creativity is connecting things." He meant that creativity comes from connecting ideas from different fields and applying those ideas to your company.

2. **Ask meaningful questions.** Steve Jobs asked, "What would the Four Seasons of retail look like?" That's an intriguing question that sparks creative answers.

3. **Craft a vision statement.** Remember, a vision is not a mission statement. A mission statement is about "us"; a vision is about "them." What are you going to do for your customers? Make sure your vision is bold, specific, concise, and consistently communicated.

CHAPTER 2

Hire for Smiles

You can dream, design and build the most wonderful place in the world, but it requires people to make the dream a reality.

—Walt Disney

The ideal Apple Store candidate knows a little about computers and a lot about people. Read the previous sentence again because it tells you everything you need to know about hiring exceptional people who will exceed the customers' expectations again and again. One Apple hiring manager told me he would prefer to hire a teacher who doesn't know computers instead of a computer expert who can't teach. Hiring the right people allows Apple managers to lead rather than dictate or manage.

Apple doesn't hire for technical knowledge. It hires for personality. Apple celebrates the diversity of the world in which we live, and nowhere is that diversity better reflected than in an Apple store. Do you have a nose ring? No problem. You're welcome at Apple. Spiked or colored hair? Again, no problem. Apple would love to have you. Do you have tattoos covering 90 percent of your body? There's a role for you at Apple. Make no mistake—it's very difficult to be hired at an Apple Store. Former head of retail Ron Johnson once said it's tougher to be hired at Apple than it is to be accepted at his alma mater, Stanford. But there are no barriers to race, sex, age, or appearance. *Apple hires for attitude and not aptitude.*

The Soul of the Apple Store

If you're looking for a "job," Apple doesn't want you. Apple prefers to hire people who hear a "calling" to apply. Apple hires people who want to play a role in creating the best-loved technology on the planet. Apple hires people who take joy in helping others discover tools they can use to change the way they live, work, and play. Apple hires enthusiastic people who want to help others achieve their dreams. It's a philosophy Steve Jobs instilled in the culture. Andy Hertzfeld, an original member of the Apple team and now an engineer at Google, once said that what Jobs taught him was to "follow your heart" and only great work comes out of doing what you adore. Hertzfeld was walking with Jobs near his home in Palo Alto, California. It was around the time the Internet bubble was minting millionaires all around them and those who weren't rich yet were talking about "exit strategies"—selling quickly for a profit. "It's such a small ambition and sad, really,"[1] Jobs said. "They should want to build something, something that lasts."

Apple creates a customer service culture that lasts because it hires for personality. The company cannot train for personality. No company can. The filtering process begins at the Apple website, which specifically states the company is only looking for people who want to change the world and who want to positively impact the lives of others: "Like when someone creates their first video with iMovie. Surfs the Internet—the real Internet—on an iPhone. Or uses the built-in iSight camera to video chat with their grandchildren. Making it all happen can be hard work. And you could probably find an easier job someplace else. But that's not the point, is it?"[2]

On the tenth anniversary of the Apple Store, the company created a poster that was circulated among its employees. It was meant to inspire employees and capture the spirit of the company. But if you read the poster carefully, it reveals much of the magic behind the brand and provides lessons for any company attempting to create a next-generation customer experience.

"At the very center of all we've accomplished are our people,"[3] the poster states.

> People who understand how important art is to technology. People who match, and often exceed, the excitement of our customers on days we release new products. The more than 30,000 smart, dedicated employees who work so hard to create lasting relationships with the millions who walk through our doors... we now see that it's our job to train our people and to learn from them. And we recruit employees with such different backgrounds—teachers, musicians, artists, engineers—that there's a lot they can teach us. We've learned how to value a magnetic personality just as much as proficiency. How to look for intelligence but give just as much weight to kindness. How to find people who want a career, not a job. And we've learned that when we hire the right people, we can lead rather than manage. We can give each person their own piece of the garden to transform.

Apple Store employees greeting customers with a warm welcome. *Source: Getty Images*

> *On the subject of best customer service—Apple rocks! Polite, efficient, bend over backward helpful.*   —Micah J.

It's Better to Be Nice than Smart

Candidates who have gone through Apple's rigorous interview process recommend that it's important to have a smile on your face and be friendly *all the time*. Be nice to everyone: employees, fellow job candidates, as well as the hiring managers. Everything is graded.

You are probably not surprised to know that restaurants, hotels, and other companies in the hospitality industry hire for attitude, but you might be surprised to learn just how much personality matters. A Cornell University study found that hospitality managers would rather hire employees with an "agreeable nature" than ones who rank higher on the "intelligent" scale.[4] When it comes to customer service, it's better to be nice than smart.

The best way to build a special workplace is to hire for attitude and train for skills, according to the *Harvard Business Review*. The research cited two companies that have built a unique and highly effective corporate culture by focusing on the type of people they hire. Arkadi Kuhlmann, founder and CEO of ING Direct, is quoted in the article. He is credited for inventing a completely new approach to banking by making it a point *not* to hire people in the banking industry. Kuhlmann noted that to truly *reenergize* an industry or a company, look outside the industry for employees. "I'd rather hire a jazz musician, a dancer, or a captain of the Israeli army. They can learn about banking. It's much more difficult for bankers to unlearn their bad habits."[5] Sounds familiar, doesn't it?

The Harvard research also points out that Southwest Airlines has prospered for forty years by embracing the hire-for-attitude philosophy. Sherry Phelps, a top executive in the Southwest Airlines People Department says, "The first thing we look for is the warrior spirit,"[6] She says, "So much of our history was born out of battles—fighting for the right to be an airline, fighting off the big guys who wanted to squash us, now fighting off the low-cost airlines trying to emulate us. We are battle-born, battle-tried people. Anyone we add has to have some of that warrior spirit." Sound familiar?

I understand what Sherry means about hiring people who fit the Southwest spirit. I fly Southwest frequently, especially on West Coast trips. On a flight from Oakland to Phoenix, one flight attendant had me and three other Gallo Communications employees roaring hysterically as he reviewed the safety instructions. Another Southwest flight attendant has become a YouTube sensation because he literally raps the lyrics to the safety instruction (some criticize this behavior, but I actually think some levity actually forces you to pay attention to the instructions instead of a dull, plodding, uninterested delivery). Southwest has built a reputation for reliable service at a good price, but it's their people who make flying a more enjoyable experience. Southwest cannot train for personality; it hires for personality.

Most corporate hiring managers and human resources (HR) professionals focus on knowledge: how much does the candidate know about the industry or product line? Apple is perfectly fine hiring a candidate who has 10 percent knowledge and 90 percent passion. I've met some employees who had never even owned a Mac product prior to applying. *Apple doesn't want to know how much you know as much as it wants to know how much you care about people.* Apple understands that a person with a lot of technical knowledge can hit the sales floor and lose customers if he or she has a lack of passion, a surly attitude, or an inability to communicate the benefits of a product clearly. Apple wants its customers to leave saying, "I just had an amazing experience. I can't wait to go home and get started!"

Shortly after leaving the journalism profession as a television anchor (and before I started my company), I worked for several years as the vice president of a global public relations agency specializing in messaging, media training, and presentation coaching. Early in my tenure at this particular PR firm, I was taken aback by a question my boss asked me in the elevator: Are you overservicing the client? Overservice? I had never heard of the word. It didn't exist in my vocabulary. I always thought PR firms were in the business of developing relationships. Clearly not. My boss had heard that for one new client—a large agribusiness company—I put in a few hours over and above what it called for in the contract. I had made the decision that our work with the client was not quite done, and I wanted to make sure they were completely satisfied with the experience.

Fast-forward four years later when I left the firm to start my own communications practice (not in the PR industry). This particular client left the PR firm because I was no longer there and has been giving my practice a substantial amount of business ever since. While reviewing our company's revenue one year, I was pleasantly surprised to see that the client—and the clients who came to us based on its recommendations—accounted for 20 percent of our revenue. Two hours of "overservice" had paid off. You see, the PR firm failed to realize that long-term relationships are based on hiring passionate employees who care about the client and who are given the freedom to satisfy the customer.

An Apple manager will rarely walk over to an employee on the sales floor and tell that person to end a conversation with a customer (unless there's a situation that requires the employee's attention, in which case the manager will make sure the customer's needs are still met). If an Apple employee spends twenty minutes talking football with a customer and five minutes talking about the product, it's perfectly OK, even if the customer doesn't leave the store having bought a product that day. Apple hires friendly employees who genuinely like people and who are passionate about building relationships. It's a philosophy that works for any company in any field.

> *Everyone is super nice at the Apple store at The Pier in Atlantic City. Take notes NJ!*   —Julia G.

Disney's People Management Philosophy

Steve Jobs was Disney's largest shareholder (today his wife Laurene Powell-Jobs manages the family's trust of 138 million Disney shares). Jobs admired the way Walt Disney built a legacy that would outlast him, and he studied how the Walt Disney company maintained a high and consistent guest experience. In turn Disney also benchmarked its customer experience against Apple. The Disney Store was reinvented with input from Steve Jobs himself. The two brands made each other better, and by studying what they've learned, your brand can become better as well.

At 60,000 employees the Walt Disney World Resort near Orlando, Florida, is the largest single-site employer in the United States. Those employees embrace the Disney culture and spread the Disney magic to the thirty million guests who visit Disney theme parks every year. I've always been fascinated with how Disney can provide a consistent guest experience in almost every customer interaction, despite thousands of guests walking through its gates each and every day. I enjoy bringing my daughters to Disneyland in Anaheim, California. As a communications specialist I experience Disney a little differently than the typical tourist. While most people are looking up at the rides, I'm looking down at the spotless grounds. Litter is almost nonexistent on Disney's Main Street or any other street in the park. The employees are friendly and outgoing, and they all have a sense of ownership over the experience each guest receives at the park. That's why they pick up litter when they see it. There's a restaurant near my office where the parking lot is always filled with cigarette butts left by employees on their breaks. Needless to say, I've never eaten there, because if the employees don't even care about the grounds, they certainly will not care about the food or the service.

Disney employees deliver a consistent experience because the organization is dedicated to a four-step approach to people management: selection, training, communication, and care. The Disney approach is worth reviewing because the steps reinforce some of the same principles behind Apple's approach to hiring, retaining, and motivating high-performing employees. These steps are well documented and transparent.

1. **Selection.** Disney shares the conditions of employment right up front. If a job candidate applies online at http://www.disneycareers .com, Disney's vision, culture, and Disney's famous appearance guidelines are clearly outlined. For people who apply in person at one of Disney's casting calls (Disney doesn't hire for jobs; it "casts" for roles), they are shown a video that explains compensation, appearance, scheduling, and transportation. Most organizations hire people who can do a job, and as a result, the

culture gets created by default. Disney and Apple *design* cultures, and they look for people who are passionate about them and who want to fit in.

2. **Training.** All new hires from cast members to senior leaders are required to spend a day at Disney University where trainers share the past, present, and future of the Disney organization. The program is called Traditions because Disney traditions and values are shared through stories, examples, and activities. The goal is to build pride in the brand. The Disney trainers who facilitate the classes are also selected more for attitude than aptitude. Sound familiar? During one period when the recession forced organizations, including Disney, to cut costs, the Traditions program was trimmed back. The reaction was immediate. Supervisors began to complain that the hiring process had been changed. Disney was hiring the same type of candidates but not putting them through a culture course. The resulting decline in customer service was so obvious, Traditions was reinstated and has remained in place ever since. Values and culture matter, but not if your team doesn't know about them.

3. **Communication.** Senior leaders at Disney have learned that trust is built through an active feedback loop with the employees responsible for delivering guest experiences. Disney leaders are encouraged to spend 60 percent of their time with employees and guests. They are constantly having conversations with employees, listening to their concerns, and taking steps to improve the experience for both internal and external customers—employees and guests. I once heard that Phil Holmes, vice president of the Magic Kingdom, posts a confidential voice message for internal employees and leaves his direct number. Holmes doesn't just tell people that he listens. He actually does. When Tim Cook took over as Apple's CEO, he, too, told employees that they could contact him at any time. One Apple Store employee told me that he sent Cook an e-mail asking a question about the signature glass doors at the entrance of his particular store. This employee was surprised to hear back from Cook, and a couple of days later an executive in Apple's retail division personally called the

employee to answer his question. With one short e-mail response to an employee's question, Cook responded, delegated, and built trust with the employee and the other staff members who heard the story.

4. **Care.** Disney provides a supportive environment where recognition and rewards play an important role in motivating and retaining high-performing employees. Disney cast members enjoy being recognized for their contributions, and leaders have devised many creative ways of doing so. We'll discuss recognition and praise a little later in Part I. For now keep in mind that Disney, Apple, and other customer service champions frequently honor the employee. One Apple Store employee told me that a few days earlier the staff had gathered for a quarterly meeting, which in most organizations is an hour or more of dull financial slides that mean more to senior leaders than to frontline staff. In this particular meeting, the management spent half an hour reviewing the numbers and the next two and a half hours celebrating the staff with games, activities, food, and even a karaoke contest. Management had turned the "meeting" into an event where the staff could interact, have fun, and bond with another.

Walt Disney believed that every employee—each cast member—must reinforce the brand's values through their conversations and actions. Disney guests should always be treated like family, and people who don't get along with the customer family have no role to play in the Disney show.

Are You Nice?

If you're looking for a critically acclaimed Italian restaurant in Chicago, you might try Spiaggia on Michigan Avenue. A Chicago favorite since 1984, Spiaggia is the winner of the James Beard Foundation award for outstanding service. What some perplexed diners have found unusual is that some waiters have exposed tattoos on their arms and don't quite fit the look one would expect at a high-end restaurant. Yet even stuffy, hard-to-please critics consider Spiaggia the best Italian restaurant in Chicago.

Andy Lansing is the president and CEO of Levy Restaurants, which owns Spiaggia and twelve other restaurants in the Chicago area. Lansing says that like Apple, Levy has a nontraditional approach to hiring. "I hire for two traits—I hire for nice and I hire for passion,"[7] he said. "If you sit down with me, no matter the position you're applying for, my first question is going to be, are you nice? The reactions are priceless. There's usually a long pause like they're waiting for me to smile. Because who asks that question? And then I say, 'No, seriously, are you nice?'" Of course, no one is going to say they're not nice. But the way a candidate answers the question and the stories they tell about the times they were nice provide Lansing with a good profile of the candidate. It also forces the candidate to go home and think about the position. If Lansing determines that a person isn't nice, it means the candidate is a wrong fit for the culture. According to Lansing, "If you have a company of nice people in a service business, that's going to be a good thing."

Lansing also asks a question that Steve Jobs had been known to ask: What are you passionate about in your life? "If this is just a job to you, it's the wrong place," says Lansing. "If you give me someone who's nice and passionate, I can teach them everything else. I don't care what school you went to, I don't care where you worked before. If you give me someone with those two traits, they will, nine out of ten times, be a great success in the company."[8]

Zane Tankel owns twenty-four Applebee's restaurants in the New York region, including the Times Square location, which has the highest annual revenue of any Applebee's in the world.

Tankel's locations generate an average annual revenue of $4.25 million, double Applebee's nationwide average. "We hire for attitude and personality,"[9] Tankel told a reporter for the *New York Times*. "We can teach you to cook, to make a drink, to be a server, but we can't teach you how to be nice." When asked how he screens for friendliness, Tankel said, "You see it in a person's demeanor and mannerisms; it's in their smile. Is it sincere? It's the way you shake my hand, look me in the eye, the way you say hello."

If you want to know what makes Apple great, Steve Jobs had an answer. "Part of what made the Macintosh great was that the people working on it were musicians and poets and artists and zoologists and historians who also happened to be the best computer scientists in the world."[10] If you hire cookie-cutter employees, you'll create a plain vanilla brand. In some cases plain vanilla might suit you just fine, and if you're happy with it, that's perfectly OK…especially with your competitors. According to Jobs's biographer Walter Isaacson, "Jobs's primary test for recruiting people in the spring of 1981 to be part of his merry band of pirates was making sure they had a passion for the product. He would sometimes bring candidates into a room where a prototype of the Mac was covered by a cloth, dramatically unveil it, and watch. If their eyes lit up, if they went right for the mouse and started pointing and clicking, Steve would smile and hire them. He wanted them to say wow!"[11]

Ron Johnson once said that Apple wants to reach your heart instead of your wallet. If you can touch your customers' hearts, profits will follow. But no company can touch hearts with heartless staff. Hire nice, friendly employees who have a passion for service and enthusiasm for your product. Hire those who say "wow!" They are the soul of your company.

CHECKOUT

1. **Visit an Apple store and watch the employees.** Take note of their personalities, watch the way they behave and interact with each other and the customers. Visit Disneyland or Disney World with kids. Take note of the smiles you see on the faces of the staff and how they interact with you, the children, and with each other.

2. **Ask yourself, "What attitudes define our best performers?"** Make an effort to build a staff of people whose attitudes reflect the culture you're trying to build. Avoid culture by default. Design a culture instead.

3. **Try asking the question of job candidates, "Are you nice?"** The way they answer the question—and how long it takes them to come up with an example—might tell you everything you need to know.

CHAPTER 3

Cultivate Fearless Employees

*If you don't feel comfortable
disagreeing, then you will
never survive.*

—Tim Cook, Apple CEO

Apple is willing to hire people based 10 percent on their knowledge and 90 percent on their personality, but employees must be *100 percent* fearless. When evaluating potential employees, Apple hiring managers will ask themselves, "Would this person have been able to go toe-to-toe with Steve Jobs?" The Apple cofounder was known for being a demanding boss, especially as it related to the customer experience, and he felt as though it was his duty to be hard on people. "I don't think I run roughshod over people, but if something sucks, I tell people to their face,"[1] Jobs told Walter Isaacson for the biography *Steve Jobs*. "It's my job to be honest.... That's the culture I tried to create. We are brutally honest with each other."

Few employees ever met Jobs in person, but if they had, would they have been able to hold their own with Steve—really go toe-to-toe with him—or would they have wilted into a blubbering mess? Apple wants employees who have a confident and fearless attitude toward customers, managers, and other superiors. The philosophy started with the most fearless employee of all—Steve Jobs himself.

Jobs's top executives understood that they had to treat Jobs with respect but that they were also expected to push back on his ideas and argue their points. "I realized very early that if you didn't voice your opinion, he would mow you down,"[2] Tim Cook told Isaacson when he was still Apple's chief operating officer. "He [Jobs] takes contrary positions to create more discussion, because it may lead to a better result. So if you don't feel comfortable disagreeing, then you'll never survive."

Although Jobs could be sharp in his criticism, his behavior was oddly inspiring because in many cases with his team, he wasn't being mean to be mean. He was challenging them to push beyond their self-perceived limits. Jobs believed that by expecting people to do great things, they would do great things. If a person was calm and confident and Jobs could see that the person was passionately devoted to the user experience, he would respect that team member and his or her opinions.

In one YouTube video that recently surfaced, Jobs is seen holding an internal meeting with employees at NeXT, the computer company he built after leaving Apple in 1985.[3] He talked about the importance of "reiterating" the vision, which he did a lot. Again, we see why all inspiring communications begin with the passionate pursuit of a bold, intoxicating vision. During the meeting, one employee took Jobs to task for a punishing production schedule. The meeting took place in 1986, and Jobs was concerned that a failure to deliver the product in the spring of 1987, eighteen months away, could lead to the company's failure. The employee argued that compromising the quality of the product to meet a subjective deadline didn't make sense. The woman was strong, forceful, articulate, and knowledgeable. Jobs looked at her, nodded, and had a comeback. The conversation grew heated but gave others the confidence to voice their opinions as well. By the end of the exchange, however, everyone was laughing, getting along, and feeling inspired about their new product.

Could You Go Toe-to-Toe with Steve Jobs?

Fearless does not mean insubordinate, obnoxious, or rude. Those are not the qualities you want to see in people on your team. According to Gary Allen, who maintains an extensive Apple Store blog, "Fearless feedback means that anyone at any level can provide constructive feedback to any other employee at any level. Not surprisingly this ties back to the original hiring process which we know focuses on creating a team, not on a person's technical skills. In the hiring phase you must evaluate whether prospective employees can both give and receive fearless feedback."[4]

How do you hire friendly, but fearless employees? A résumé will not reveal fearlessness. A traditional job interview with contrived questions like, "What's your greatest weakness?" will not reveal fearlessness. True confidence is revealed through conversations with hiring managers and employees.

"First and foremost, Apple is looking for a 'type,' not a person with vast experience and knowledge," says Gary Allen. "If you are a team player and can fit into Apple's work ethic and philosophy, the company will teach you anything you need to know to meet their job performance goals. You do not need retailing or computer repair experience to be hired." You do, however, need passion, spirit, and a collaborative attitude.

Apple has a three-step hiring process that can last more than one month. A description of each step in the process follows.

Step One

The first step is to put a group of candidates in a room with other candidates, hiring managers, and Apple Store employees. According to Allen, the interviews are very informal and there does not seem to be a standard set of questions for the interview. Sometimes candidates are asked simple questions such as, "What is your favorite ice cream?" These questions are meant to see who speaks up, how well they project, and how confident they are in front of others. Wallflowers are quickly weeded out. The larger group is broken up into smaller groups of about four to five people and asked questions about how they would respond to a potential situation: for example, a customer comes in with an iPhone that doesn't work. How would the candidates handle it? The answer is less important than how the candidate arrived at the answer. A "know-it-all" might not last to the next round. The person who doesn't know the answer but who interacted with the group and even asked for help is the one who stands out. Apple is looking for people who exhibit the traits of a team player. A very small percentage of the larger group gets called back for step two in the hiring—or the weeding out—process. One applicant who went through the process posted this description on his blog:

> The meeting was held at an Apple store after it had closed for the day. There were about twenty applicants there. Once we had all arrived, store management performed introductions and told us they were going to be hiring some of us to fill various positions. We were asked to go around the room, introduce ourselves, tell why we wanted to work for Apple, and something unique or interesting about ourselves. Next, they surprised us by giving us five minutes to create an "About Me" page in Pages that included a picture of ourselves. At this point I was feeling pretty good because I have quite a bit of experience with Pages and most of the people there, even though they had called themselves Mac fanatics not ten minutes ago, barely even knew what Pages was.[5]

Now think about what had just happened. Ten minutes earlier some people in the room were bragging about how much technical knowledge they had about Macs and the programs. But recruiters were not looking for technical know-how; they were looking for confident team players who were also humble enough to acknowledge what they didn't know. Fearlessness is not arrogance. Arrogance covers up insecurities. Fearless applicants speak up in a group without trying to impress the group with how much they know.

Step Two

Step two involves candidates sitting in front of a five-member panel made up of managers, trainers, and employees who work in the "red zone," the front part of the store where the sales take place. Again, the panel will ask some technical questions, but it's perfectly fine if the candidate doesn't know all the answers. Apple customers are demanding. It's nearly impossible to predict all of their questions and concerns. An arrogant candidate stands little chance of getting through the next round. The panel is looking for some technical knowledge, the confidence to ask for help, and the commitment to make sure the customer walks out of the store with a smile on his or her face. Managers are judging whether the candidate can go toe-to-toe with Steve Jobs, but they also want to determine that the potential employee can offer a Ritz-Carlton level of customer service.

Step Three

Candidates who make it to round three have a good chance of being hired. Managers might bring a candidate to the third round simply to reassure themselves and their staff that the new employee has passion and the right attitude. If you're knowledgeable but lacking in passion, you might not make it to the Apple sales floor. In this stage a candidate might be asked questions about her success in a previous job. Again, the answer is not as important as the way the question is answered. A candidate who takes all the credit for his success will not be as impressive as the person who credits the team. "More than anything, this personal interview attempts to judge your suitability to the team, not your technical or sales skills," says Allen.

Apple CEO Tim Cook shined under Jobs because, according to Walter Isaacson, he was "calm and decisive when in command, but he didn't seek any notice or acclaim for himself."[6]

Apple employees have confidence in themselves and are self-assured enough to ask for help when they don't know the answer to a question. Going toe-to-toe with Steve Jobs simply means that an employee believes in something and is willing to fight for it. Some hiring managers at Apple will purposely disagree with a candidate's opinion even if the hiring manager involved completely agrees. They are looking for fearlessness. Does the candidate get rattled? Does he or she fold? Again, they are not looking for people who have all the answers, but people who will defend their point and not be shy to ask for help when they need it.

In 1981 the original Macintosh team gave out awards to people who best stood up to Steve Jobs. According to Isaacson, "If you were calmly confident, if Jobs sized you up and decided that you knew what you were doing, he would respect you. In both his personal and professional life over the years, his inner circle tended to include many more strong people than toadies."[7] Don't hire toadies. Hire fearless employees instead.

Fearless Employees Take Ownership

What does fearlessness look like on the sales floor? In a word—ownership. You'll notice something on the Apple sales floor that is highly unusual in other retailers. If you approach an employee with a problem or question, the employee must own the problem and see that you are cared for. This tactic rarely happens anywhere else. I once approached a friend who looked very tired and agitated. She had just returned from a "big box" electronics retailer to buy a wireless router. "I'm furious," she said. "I stood there for ten minutes and four different people—four people—all told me that 'it's not my department.' They literally just walked away leaving me to figure it out for myself." This would never happen in an Apple Store, and it would never happen in a Four Seasons. Both brands hire friendly, but fearless employees who take ownership of the problem and will not let it rest until the customer gets resolution. Cowardly employees will pass the buck. Fearless employees ask for help if they don't have the answers. A fearless employee owns the relationship from beginning to end. No obstacle will get in the way of creating a satisfying relationship between the customer and the brand.

> *Apple, your products are expensive and your shops a bit weird, but I love your customer service.* —John S.

Don't Ask What Steve Would Do, Do What Is Right

Fearless employees do the right thing for the customer, and they do right for the team. Shortly before his death, Steve Jobs said he didn't want Apple employees to ask, "What would Steve do?" Instead he wanted them to do what's right. Former Boston Red Sox manager Terry Francona agrees with that philosophy. "I really care about having an atmosphere where my players care about doing the right thing,"[8] Francona said shortly after leading the Red Sox to the World Series Championship in 2004, the first time the club had won a World Series in eighty-six years. "For me it would be silly to walk around like a drill sergeant," said Francona. Instead Francona cultivated a clubhouse culture where, despite some big egos, players understood the ultimate direction of the team, respected each other, and were confident about doing what's right for the team instead of gratifying their own egos. The players respected their coach and were fiercely loyal to each other on the field.

When you create an atmosphere where good players want to do the right thing—in retail or in sports—it doesn't guarantee that you will win "the championship," but it will guarantee that you are putting your team in the best position to win.

A Fearless Fit

The clothing store chain Men's Wearhouse has fostered what it calls a "fearless and energized workplace." During a one-day trip to Los Angeles to meet with a client, an *ABC News* producer called me unexpectedly to schedule an important interview that would air on a national program. I had not packed a suit or a tie for this trip, and I really felt like the topic required more formal attire. So I did what thousands of other men must have done that day—dropped into a Men's Wearhouse to buy some nice-fitting clothes that look good without breaking the bank. I purchased two coats and two ties, all while the car was waiting outside. The driver didn't have to wait long. It took all of fifteen minutes from the time I entered the store.

As soon as I walked into the store I talked to the first salesperson I saw, Sam. I told Sam my predicament, and Sam, being a fearless employee, said, "I don't even have to measure you. You're a 42 regular. Come this way. I know exactly what you need." Sam realized we didn't have time for small talk. His goal was to satisfy the customer and to make him look his best, all in fifteen minutes.

The Men's Wearhouse hires for fearlessness. According to the store's philosophy, "The emotional atmosphere within a retail store environment can make or break that store's ability to reach its financial goals. Store appearance and product knowledge are certainly important, but customer comfort and satisfaction during the shopping experience hinge on something else: our store must feel emotionally energized."[9] Store appearance plays a critical role at Apple, but it's the experience that customers have in the store with employees that makes the difference for Apple, Men's Wearhouse, or any other retailer known for exceptional customer service.

Where does the positive shopping experience start? Each team member must feel good about being part of the team—the "corporate tribe"—at Men's Wearhouse. "We encourage employees to communicate directly to their managers—or go higher, if necessary—when fairness and respect are compromised." It's equally important to let employees make decisions they feel are in the best interest of the customer—in sports it's the equivalent of a quarterback calling an "audible" when he believes it's the right play to run even though it wasn't the play the coach called. "Mistakes are opportunities for both mentoring and learning. Reducing fear draws out our employees' best efforts and most positive attitudes."

Fear Destroys Culture

Fear inhibits leadership, destroys cultures, and ultimately leads to a poor customer experience. One study found that in a recession only half of employees in the United States took all their vacation time (in a country where the average vacation is only two weeks).[10] When employees were asked why they didn't take their vacation, many expressed the fear of becoming targets in the next round of layoffs. These "fearful" employees come to work tired, irritated, and uninspired because they haven't had a chance to recharge or explore new ideas. Expecting these employees to provide an exceptional customer service is like asking the cast of *Jersey Shore* to go one day without making fools of themselves. It's not going to happen. Fear also leads to something even more damaging to creating a customer-centered culture. Scared employees are reluctant to speak up, and if they do not voice their opinions, it's nearly impossible to offer feedback. Feedback, as you'll learn in the next chapter, is a key ingredient in Apple's secret sauce.

> *I love the Apple Store at FL's Millenia Mall! Super helpful & great customer service.* —Deb S.

The Crazy Ones

When Steve Jobs returned to rescue Apple in 1997, he didn't have any new products to announce (the breakthroughs would begin the following year with the introduction of the iMac). Instead, Jobs motivated his team by creating a television ad—not for his customers, but for his employees. Jobs wrote the words to *The Crazy Ones* because he wanted to remind employees of Apple's core values and beliefs. The words came from the bottom of Steve's soul. During the celebration of Steve's life on October 19, 2011, at the Apple campus, Tim Cook played a version of the ad that he himself had heard for the first time after Steve's death. Richard Dreyfus was the actor who voiced the final television ad, but Cook played the version Jobs read in his own voice.

> Here's to the crazy ones. The misfits. The rebels. The troublemakers. The round pegs in the square holes. The ones who see things differently. They're not fond of rules and they have no respect for the status quo. You can quote them, disagree with them, glorify or vilify them. About the only thing you can't do is ignore them, because they change things. They push the human race forward. While some may see them as the crazy ones, we see genius. Because the people who are crazy enough to think they can change the world are the ones who do.[11]

Steve Jobs was fearless, and he hired employees who shared his attitude.

Jony and Steve's Dopey Ideas

On Wednesday, October 19, 2011, Apple closed all of its retail locations for two hours so employees could attend a "Celebration of Steve's Life" broadcast live from the Apple headquarters in Cupertino, California. Jonathan "Jony" Ive was one of the speakers. Jobs called Ive his "spiritual partner" at Apple. Both men loved design and would speak daily about creating products that were simple, elegant, and easy to use. As Apple's head of design, Ive is largely responsible for designing some of the most innovative technology products on the planet—iPod, Macbook, iPhone, and iPad.

Ive was invited to say a few words at the memorial celebration. "Steve used to say to me—and he used to say it a lot—hey, Jony, here's a dopey idea,"[12] Ive told the audience. "And sometimes they were. Sometimes they were truly dreadful. But sometimes they took the air from the room and left us both completely silent: bold, crazy, magnificent ideas or quiet, simple ones which, in their subtlety, their detail, were truly profound." Jobs loved the process of creativity and approached it with a "rare and wonderful reverence," according to Ive. Jobs pitched "dopey" ideas, and he expected people to give him open, honest feedback. He could also be harsh with Ive, but he expected Ive to defend his ideas. Both men cherished the process and realized that innovation cannot flourish without the open exchange of ideas and feedback. But without fearlessness, the process breaks down.

In remembering Jobs, Ive said, "He better than anyone understood that while ideas ultimately could be so powerful, they begin as fragile, barely formed thoughts, so easily missed, so easily compromised, so easily squished." Ive thrived for more than ten years under Jobs because he was fearless. He wasn't a wallflower. Ive pitched ideas passionately even though he knew there would be a good chance Jobs might cut them down with a curt, harsh rejection. But he had the confidence to go toe-to-toe with Jobs.

CHECKOUT

1. **Go toe-to-toe with Jobs.** When evaluating potential talent, ask yourself, "Would this person have gone toe-to-toe with Steve Jobs, or would he or she have been mowed over?"

2. **Provide Ritz-Carlton customer service.** If your job candidate passes the first question, ask yourself a second, "Is this person capable of providing Ritz-Carlton level customer service with the right training?"

3. **Encourage team interaction.** Don't hire anyone without seeing how the person interacts with others. Is the person a know-it-all, or does he or she treat others with respect and even ask for help from time to time?

CHAPTER 4

Build Trust

*Trust men and they will be true
to you; treat them greatly and they
will show themselves great.*

—Ralph Waldo Emerson

Apple does not like to hire arrogant techies who think they know it all, because as star employees will tell you, you can't know everything. Just when you think you have it figured out, the demanding Apple customer will throw you a question, concern, or situation you simply haven't prepared to address. The goal is not to impress customers with knowledge. The goal is to leave customers feeling special and to enrich their lives.

Apple looks for personality and for those who can handle "ambiguity." If an employee has internalized the vision, knows the messaging, has engaged in fearless feedback, and trusts her team and her managers, she will be much more effective in dealing with unexpected questions, demands, and concerns. She will confidently make on-the-spot decisions for the good of the customer relationship.

Building a Trusting Relationship

Although Apple does not require that its managers read *Speed of Trust* by Stephen M. R. Covey, I've met several managers who are familiar with Covey's thirteen behaviors of "high-trust leaders" and try to instill these behaviors in their teams. "The ability to establish, grow, extend, and restore trust with all stakeholders is the key leadership competency of the new, global economy,"[1] writes Covey.

According to research cited in Covey's book, only 51 percent of employees have trust and confidence in senior management, and only 36 percent believe their leaders act with honesty and integrity. A low-trust environment is a recipe for disaster. "Low trust causes friction, whether it is caused by unethical behavior or by ethical but incompetent behavior,"[2] says Covey. "Low trust is the greatest cost in life and in organizations. Low trust creates hidden agendas, politics, interpersonal conflict, interdepartmental rivalries, win-lose thinking, defensive and protective communication. Low trust slows everything—every decision, every communication, and every relationship."

Apple managers work hard at building and maintaining trust and, yes, restoring trust when it is lost. Managers strive to create a trusting environment where employees feel confident giving and receiving feedback and making their customers feel valued. Here are Covey's thirteen trust behaviors with explanations and how they apply to the Apple experience. If you do not practice these behaviors as a leader in your organization, you might want to start. You will never develop an exceptional customer service strategy without developing trust.

Talk Straight

Straight-talking managers let employees know where they stand, and they use simple, clear directions. Remember the question that hiring managers at Apple ask themselves: can this person go toe-to-toe with Steve Jobs? Jobs appreciated creative ideas. His first response might have been "It's shit"; but after thinking about it, Jobs would come around to good ideas. Isaacson confirms that Jobs allowed, even encouraged, people to challenge him. Although employees could challenge Jobs, he demanded clarity from the conversation. Obfuscation was a direct path to getting fired or getting your head bitten off. If a fearless Apple store employee believes it's in the best interest of the company and its long-term relationship with a customer to replace a broken device that is past the warranty period, the employee might win the argument. But he had better have a good reason he can articulate simply and clearly to his manager.

Straight talk also applies to the interaction between employee and customer. If a customer wants to save $200 by purchasing a computer with less power, but the Apple salesperson knows—after asking probing questions—that the customer will regret the decision, the salesperson must speak clearly and bluntly. For example, a straight-talking salesperson might say something like, "I'm not on commission, and I'll sell you that machine if it's what you want. But I'm letting you know, based on what you've told me, that you'll be back here to buy a new computer in two years. But if you spend $200 more today, you'll have no problem for the next five years."

Demonstrate Respect

A respectful manager genuinely cares about her employees and her customers. She respects the dignity of everyone on the team. Steve Jobs surrounded himself with a small group of A-players. But in a retail environment with 35,000 employees, the reality is that some B-players will also be on the sales floor. Managers must show kindness and respect to everyone on the team, even a player who is not living up to his potential. Employees have a way of raising their game when they are given praise and positive feedback and are treated with dignity.

Create Transparency

Transparent managers are open and authentic. They disclose information if the information improves the customer experience, and they expect the same from their employees. For example, one fearless Apple manager asked an employee how things were going on the floor. The employee responded, "Fine." The manager asked the question again and added, "Be open and honest." The manager got an earful, but it was feedback he needed to hear.

An employee also needs to trust a manager enough to be open. A specialist on a busy Apple floor might have to say, "I'm overwhelmed in this section right now." The manager can replace that person in the section, move the person to another section, or give the person the right tools or resources needed to serve the customer better. But if the employee doesn't trust the manager, the employee might stew about it and get frustrated, which could lead to deteriorating customer interactions. You will learn more about developing an effective feedback loop, which is a result of established trust, in Chapter 5.

Right Wrongs

Managers who right wrongs apologize quickly. They don't let pride get in the way of doing the right thing. Everything in an Apple Store is about creating "promoters," customers who are so happy they will recommend Apple products to their friends. Anything that gets in the way of that relationship must be addressed quickly. If a manager mistakenly criticizes an employee or, because he's human, is having a bad day, it's up to the manager to clear his head and apologize for his behavior. Righting a wrong quickly and authentically will restore trust among the team and even add a reservoir of trust that could benefit a supervisor in the future.

Show Loyalty

Loyal managers freely give credit to others and acknowledge the contribution of others. If they promise something, they follow through. They don't break the trust. I spoke to the CEO of Griffin Hospital in Derby, Connecticut. Griffin is consistently ranked as one of the best places to work in the country. The hospital has committed itself to open and honest communications between management and staff. That commitment was put to the test in November 2001, when the first victim of what would become a deadly, nationwide anthrax attack was brought to the hospital. The governor of the state called the CEO, Patrick Charmel, and urged him to keep it quiet. Charmel had scheduled a staff meeting where he had planned to disclose the information. Despite admonitions from politicians and even the FBI, Charmel told his staff. He trusted them to keep the news confidential until it was made public. Charmel's staff honors his loyalty every day by maintaining the highest standards of customer satisfaction in the healthcare industry.

Deliver Results

A manager who delivers results accomplishes what he is hired to do. He makes things happen. If he should fail to meet a deadline or make a goal, he doesn't blame his team. The buck stops with him and he takes the hit. After a disheartening loss for the San Francisco 49ers in the 2011 season, new coach Jim Harbaugh told the assembled press that the blame rested with him. He didn't blame the players or the conditions. He had not prepared them enough for the defense they would face. In the first nine games of the year, Harbaugh had built a tremendous reservoir of trust and respect among his players. He wasn't going to deplete that reservoir by assigning blame to anyone but himself. The 49ers reached the playoffs that season for the first time since 2002, losing the NFC title game in overtime. Many of the players said that Harbaugh was the most inspiring coach they had played for. In sports and in business, players need to trust their leader.

Get Better

Managers who get better are constantly soliciting feedback, reading books, and learning new skills to keep up with the pace of change in today's world. When Apple sends out a customer survey, its stores are "growing." When an Apple Store manager asks employees for feedback, he's growing. Apple managers are urged to tackle the sixty-seven leadership competencies discussed in the Korn/Ferry book, *FYI: For Your Improvement.* Some Apple Stores have several copies of the book available for their staff. No one expects an employee to master all sixty-seven competencies, but they are encouraged to improve in one or two areas a year as part of their ongoing personal and professional development.

Confront Reality

A manager who confronts reality tackles tough issues head-on. She doesn't let things fester. She shares bad news as well as the good news. She's also quick to address "opportunities" to improve customer interaction. (Apple Retail employees seem to avoid the word *problem.*) For example, if a manager sees that an employee had a difficult time with a customer, she might address the situation by asking, "Can you tell me about that experience? I'd like to know your perspective, and then I'll tell what I saw. Together we can work at creating an opportunity to enhance the customer experience." Avoiding the word *problem* or other negative words helps establish trust, which will encourage the employee to provide feedback and communicate more openly (as you will learn more about in Chapter 5).

Clarify Expectations

Trustworthy managers disclose expectations right at the start. They never assume that everyone knows what's expected of them. Apple employees know that they are expected to walk through the Apple five steps of service (discussed in Part II).

Expectations must be set for customers, as well. For example, customers will often show up at the Genius Bar at an Apple Store to ask questions or have repairs made. If they show up without an appointment, an Apple employee might set expectations: "We can accommodate you this time, but if you come in next time without an appointment, we might not be as lucky. Do you know how to make an appointment online? If not, I'd be glad to show you." I've seen customers walk into an Apple Store and complain that they can't get served immediately (or they voice their complaint on their social networks, like Twitter and Facebook). I believe that if these customers had been served before without having expectations set for next time, they come to expect immediate service and they get angry if they don't get it. Setting proper expectations can resolve these types of issues.

As discussed earlier, Disney is another brand known for creating a unique customer experience. Both Apple and Disney hire for attitude and personality, but both brands have very different expectations when it comes to a person's appearance. According to Disney's website, its Walt Disney parks have become famous for a friendly, classic appearance—the Disney look. The look is clean, natural, and unpolished and avoids cutting-edge trends or extremes. The Disney website has a long list of requirements that covers body alterations, hair, fingernails, and makeup. If you don't care to adhere to the requirements, you need not apply. The expectations are clearly spelled out.

Practice Accountability

Accountable managers take responsibility for their section of the sales floor or their team members. They do not blame others when things go wrong. They take full responsibility for the behavior of their employees in a sales environment. Billionaire Warren Buffett once said that "when the tide goes out you see who's swimming naked." The same holds true for quarterly goals. When goals are missed, you see which leaders are fearless and trustworthy and which are spineless and untrustworthy. I recall working for a PR firm during one bad quarter when all the senior leaders started pointing the finger at each other and individual units within the department. It was discouraging and disheartening. Not surprisingly, the PR firm soon became known for uninspiring managers and disappointed clients. I left when I realized the firm did not meet my internal standards for excellence. Many of the other A-players left as well in the months to follow. People who are at the top of their game want to work for leaders whom they trust and admire.

Listen First

Managers who listen take proactive steps to understand the needs and desires of their internal and external stakeholders: employees and customers. The Apple credo card states, "We value each customer problem as an opportunity to shine. We listen and respond immediately to all feedback, taking personal initiative to make it right. We encourage open dialogue with our people and customers to share ideas about improving our stores, our processes, and our performance."[3]

Some Apple managers whom I've met are very humble when it comes to this trust component. "We don't get caught up in the illusion that we know everything or have all the right answers." In Part II, you will learn about the Apple five steps of service. Step four is to "listen" for any unresolved issues, concerns, or questions.

Keep Commitments

Managers who keep their commitments do what they say they are going to do. If a manager promises an employee that he will address a concern at the end of the shift, he'd better keep that commitment. Managers who overpromise and underdeliver will lose the trust of their team very quickly. This point goes with delivering results: managers who can deliver results are more likely going to follow through with their commitments.

Extend Trust

Fearless managers extend trust. They don't withhold trust because some risk is involved. Of course, they are careful, but they demonstrate a propensity to trust their employees. Covey offers the following advice: "Extend trust abundantly to those who have earned your trust. Extend conditionally to those who are earning your trust."[4] According to Covey, trust means confidence. The opposite of trust—distrust—is suspicion. "When you trust people, you have confidence in them, in their integrity, and in their abilities." Trust is established when everyone on the team—the newbie, the part-timer, the veteran, feels like an important part of the team. "Smart leaders create an environment that encourages appropriate risk-taking, an environment that makes it safe to make mistakes," says Covey.

The fastest way to lose trust—at Apple or any other company— is to violate these thirteen principles. Trust will be shattered if a manager fails to speak clearly, seeks personal gain at the expense of the team, withholds information, distorts information, or refuses to listen.

Integrity and Trust: Nothing Else Matters

Integrity and trust together are an important competency in the Lominger Korn/Ferry leadership system applied at Apple and many other brands. "Integrity and trust are on almost every success profile we see. It is a basic threshold requirement to be a part of the team. Without it, almost nothing else matters."[5] The Lominger system recommends that if people don't buy what you're saying, you might want to try the following remedies. Note how closely these remedies follow the guidelines offered in Covey's *Speed of Trust*:

- **Say what needs to be said.** Don't hold back and qualify everything you say. Speak up when it's the right thing to do.

- **Don't exaggerate or overpromise.** Don't commit to too many things. Don't embellish and stretch the truth.

- **Keep confidences.** Don't reveal personal information given to you in confidence.

- **Take responsibility.** Don't look for others to blame.

- **Step up to address issues.** Don't say things just to get along and to avoid trouble.

- **Share information.** Don't hold back critical information.

- **Follow through.** Don't avoid following through, especially on simple commitments.

- **Put the team first.** Don't use *I* instead of *we*. Signal that you are thinking as a team.

In many ways, trust is the hardest concept to convey, and yet it's also the easiest if you cut to the essence of what it means to be a trustworthy leader. Virgin entrepreneur Richard Branson might have said it best: "I try to treat people as human beings...if they know you care, it brings out the best in them."[6] Show your team that you care. Once you have clearly shown this, it will be easier to have open communication with them, and they will want to give you feedback that continues to keep the customer experience as memorable as it should be every time.

CHECKOUT

1. **Invest in a copy of *FYI* by Lominger Korn/Ferry.** It's a development guide for learners, managers, mentors, and feedback givers. Study competency 29, Integrity and Trust.

2. **Read *Speed of Trust* by Stephen M. R. Covey.** It will give you another opportunity to explore the thirteen habits of trustworthy leaders and apply the habits to yourself and your team.

3. **Make your approach more receptive and open.** Avoid using the pronoun *I* when addressing issues that need change. Stay away from labeling experiences or issues as "problems." Listen first. Changing habits take effort and focus, but it's never too late to evolve the way you do things.

CHAPTER 5

Foster a Feedback Loop

See feedback as a gift.
—Apple tenth anniversary poster

S teve Jobs didn't rely on focus groups, because he believed that people did not know what they wanted until you showed them. In some cases this was very true. Would you have agreed to pay ninety-nine cents a song in 2003 when you could otherwise download songs on the Internet for free? But Jobs realized what most people did not—music fans would pay for a better, seamless, and legal customer experience. In January 2010, would you have told Jobs that you wanted to carry around yet another device in addition to a mobile phone and a laptop computer? Jobs realized that people really wanted an ultra-portable device that would make it easier to do e-mail, browse the Internet, and enjoy photographs, video, and books. Nobody asked for the iPad, but they couldn't buy enough of them. When it came to big innovations, Jobs did indeed rely on his intuition and imagination. But it is incorrect to assume that Apple never listens to its customer. The exact opposite is true. Apple listens to its customers all the time and more important, actively solicits feedback from both its internal customers (employees) and external customers.

Feedback requires fearlessness and trust. That's why fearlessness and trust come before feedback as far as the principles discussed in this book. A fearful employee will be unwilling to be open and honest in offering feedback about the company, its policies, or a manager. A fearful manager who hasn't instilled trust will be defensive and unwilling to listen to constructive input.

Fearless employees will disagree with you, but they will offer valuable feedback when the opportunity presents itself. I read a story about Emma Sky, a British pacifist who was dedicated to getting the United States out of Iraq. In 2007 she became a key aide to General Ray Ordierno, the former commanding general of the U.S. forces in Iraq. The tiny British woman and the general (Ordierno is 6 feet, 5 inches) made an odd-looking pair, but she played an outsized role—she actively disagreed with Ordierno. She was assigned the role purposely to disagree with him! Ordierno is "fearless."

"Leaders who solicit opinions from people who disagree with them are smart enough to realize that they do not have all the answers,"[1] says leadership consultant John Baldoni. "Such leaders also must make it safe for others to disagree: otherwise the exercise is moot." Baldoni recommends that companies hire employees who exhibit "character." In Baldoni's definition, character is a willingness to do what's right for the team and the courage to stand up for ideas. Apple certainly looks for character. Steve Jobs admonished his employees not to do what they think "Steve would do" but to do what's right for the team. Apple managers also look for people who can stand up for their ideas, who could go toe-to-toe with Steve Jobs because they must be brave enough to voice their opinions. The Apple experience doesn't work without feedback. Steve Jobs believed so much in feedback—internal and external—he would periodically pick up the phone at Apple customer care. He wanted to hear directly from customers about their frustrations. Jobs didn't believe the customer was always right. In fact, he could shoot down a customer with a pointed word or phrase. But more often than not, Jobs sought feedback, listened, and like any good leader, acted on that feedback. He saw feedback as a gift.

> *I've just experienced the most exceptional customer service in the Exeter Apple Store. Quite amazing. I'm still stunned.*
>
> —Richard C.

Fearless Feedback

Feedback is a critical component behind Apple's customer service excellence. *Feedback* is one of the most common words that I hear from Apple Store employees. Apple managers cultivate an open-door policy where employees feel comfortable and empowered to make comments and suggestions. But it works both ways. Employees and managers must be fearless in their pursuit of feedback. For example, after making a sale, a typical (nonfearless) employee would unlikely ask for feedback, and if he did, he might ask a meek question such as, "How did I do?" This typically leads to an equally empty, unsatisfying, and uninstructive answer: "Fine." A fearless employee will dig deeper: "Where did I miss an opportunity? On a scale of 1 to 10, where do I rank in terms of customer engagement? Did I do everything possible to create a customer for life?"

Feedback is best given when the interaction is still fresh in everyone's mind. Not always, but frequently, it is given soon after a sales transaction in an Apple Store. Managers will ask probing questions to help employees build better quality relationships with customers. They will ask questions such as, "What was the experience like? What did you miss? How could the transaction have been different?" Managers are not expected to hold a customer service training class after every transaction, but simply asking these questions will help an employee be present the next time she's with a customer.

The immediate feedback loop can help any brand create a richer, more satisfying experience between staff and customers. The Apple philosophy applies to any business, in any industry. For example, most employees working behind the counter of an ice cream store want nothing more than to scoop an ice cream into a cone and get the customer on his way before it melts. But a fearless feedback loop will greatly improve the quality of the employee's next interaction.

The Apple approach would be for the manager to ask probing questions of the employee: "What other experiences did you introduce to the customer? Did you ask, 'What do you normally order when you come here?' Did you recommend anything based on the customer's requests or desires?" This feedback could lead to a richer experience because the frontline employee will be more involved in building relationships. The next conversation might go like this:

> **Employee:** Welcome to Yummy Ice Cream. We're glad you're here.
>
> **Customer:** It's hot out there! I'm not surprised that you have a line out the door.
>
> **Employee:** It sure is. I hear it's going to be close to 100 degrees today. We certainly have some great flavors to help cool you down. Tell me, what's your favorite ice cream?
>
> **Customer:** I know it's simple, but I really like vanilla.
>
> **Employee:** Awesome. I love vanilla, too. Have you tried Cherries Jubilee? It's a vanilla-based ice cream with a twist—we add chocolate and cherries. Not only that, it's served in our waffle cones, which are unique because we make them all by hand every morning, right here in the store.
>
> **Customer:** Sounds good. I'm not a huge fan of cherries, but I like the idea of chocolate and the waffle cone. Let's do that. Thanks.

At this point it won't matter to the customer that the ice cream treat he did buy cost three dollars more than the vanilla cone. He did learn something new, his eyes were opened to a new flavor combination, and he enjoyed the relationship that began to form, just in a few short seconds.

We will discuss "probing" questions in Part II, but for now just pay attention to the fact that the employee in the ice cream example connected a recommendation to the customer's likes. The employee didn't say, "Oh, you like vanilla. Have you tried mocha?" The same applies to the auto industry. If a car buyer walks in and starts talking about her three children and family trips, an astute car salesman won't point her to a two-seater turbo. When I walked into an Apple Store to shop for a new iPod, the specialist didn't try to sell me a

Macbook Air. But he did introduce me to the iPod Touch because after asking probing questions, he learned that I like some music apps like Pandora. The iPod Touch, he said, would give me all the benefits and apps of an iPhone, without the phone. The Apple specialist had learned—through training and constant feedback—how to create an enriching experience for his customer.

In another situation, I entered an Apple Store specifically to purchase a new notebook computer. The Specialist who worked with me, "Carla," was one of the most enthusiastic people I had ever encountered at any retail store. Carla was a middle-aged woman who was clearly a free spirit. She had a purple streak in her hair and wore a beret. She made the buying experience a real pleasure. Of course, the journalist in me came out, and I asked her as many questions as she asked me.

"How long have you been working here?" I asked.

"Only six months."

"Did you work in another retail store? A technology company?" I asked. "You seem to know a lot about operating systems."

"It's funny," she said. "I had never worked in retail, and I didn't know much about computers. But I *loved* Apple products. I had taken some One to One classes, and my goal is to be a Creative (Creatives are the instructors who teach personalized classes in the store). I remember there were about one hundred people in my first interview. A few were arrogant and thought they'd nail the job because they knew so much about Apple products. But Apple is different. They weren't looking for technical knowledge. They hire for passion and personality. I'm really proud to work for a company that cares about its customers."

"I can see that," I responded. "You could have fooled me. I would have thought that you've been selling Apple products your whole life."

"I've been here six months, and I still get feedback every day. We have discussions at the end of every shift. I'll tell them all about this lovely interaction. Thanks for coming in and making my day!"

Carla made me feel good. I had a smile on my face, and I couldn't believe how outgoing and friendly she was. Carla represents the next generation of customer service. But if it wasn't for the consistent feedback Carla—a Specialist—received from her manager, her natural friendliness would not have been channeled into creating a strategic advantage in the industry.

> I must say, the customer service at Apple is great. They really helped me get everything I needed for my purchase.
> —Stephen M.

The Ultimate Question

One reason why Apple scores higher than most other retailers on every metric (visitors, revenue per square foot, employee retention, etc.) is feedback. Interestingly, when you ask the casual Apple Store customers why they were satisfied with their experience, they will rarely, if ever, mention the word *feedback*. Conduct a Twitter search for Apple and customer service, and you will find dozens of enthusiastic customers who are sharing their positive experiences with friends on their larger social networks. Add the word *feedback* to the search term and no results will show up. Yet feedback is Apple's under-the-hood philosophy that guides nearly everything Apple does, and it's a key component in cultivating an engaging team.

Apple uses the Net Promoter Score (NPS) to "monitor the employee and customer experience and to identify and address where we can better serve."[2] The NPS score measures engagement. Studies have consistently shown that companies with higher levels of employee and customer engagement outperform their peers on the stock market and other metrics of financial success. But recall from the earlier Gallup research that a full 70 percent of employees in the United States are either "not engaged" or "fully disengaged."[3]

In 2003, Fred Reichheld, a partner at Bain & Company, created a new way to measure customer relationships. He called it the Net Promoter Score. But as thousands of companies adopted the score, they expanded it, customized it, or improved the methodology. The result is an NPS that thousands of companies, including Apple, use to measure customer loyalty and to transform their organizations.

Companies like Apple use NPS to ask two important questions, one aimed at internal "customers"—employees—and the other at external customers. The question asked of employees is "On a 0-to-10 scale, how likely is it that you would recommend us as a place to work?"[4] The question asked of customers—the ultimate question to gauge customer engagement—"On a 0-to-10 scale, how likely is it that you would recommend us (or this product/service/brand) to a friend or colleague?" Respondents to these questions fall into three categories:

1. **Promoters.** These are loyal enthusiasts who keep buying from a company and urge their friends to do the same. In response to the question, "How likely are you to recommend products and services to a friend," promoters are those who respond with a 9 or 10. They are saying that their experience with your brand has enriched their lives.

2. **Passives.** These are satisfied customers who are easily wooed by the competition. If a competitor can shave a few bucks off the price of a product, the passives are all over it.

3. **Detractors.** These folks bring down the total score and do a lot of damage. They are unhappy customers who feel badly mistreated. They cut back on their purchases, switch to the competition if they can, and share their negative experience on Twitter, Facebook, foursquare, and other social media platforms. "Customers who feel ignored or mistreated find ways to get even. They drive up service costs by reporting numerous problems. They demoralize frontline employees with their complaints and demands. They gripe to friends, relatives, colleagues—anyone who will listen. Detractors tarnish a firm's reputation and diminish its ability to recruit the best employees and customers."[5]

NPS is measured by taking the percent of customers who are promoters (P) and subtracting the percentage who are detractors (D).

$$P - D = NPS$$

The average company sputters along with an NPS rating of 5 to 10 percent (some even have negative ratings, which means there are more detractors than promoters). Many brands admired for their service, like Southwest Airlines, fall in the 60 percent range. But the real standouts—net promoters—such as Apple, Amazon, Costco, Trader Joe's, or USAA in the financial services industry, push the NPS score to more than 80 percent. That's the equivalent word-of-mouth of nine people talking up the service to their friends while only one person is feeling let down. I've talked to individual Apple managers who say they only want to see nine or ten. Anything less is considered a failure and requires corrective action immediately.

Apple has been using the NPS feedback loop for years to improve the way they do business—to create a team of employees who love working for the company and to cultivate a group of loyal customers who sing their praises. Everyone is focused on one goal: treat customers so well those customers become loyal promoters of the brand. "NPS was a natural fit for Apple,"[6] said former Apple head of retail Ron Johnson. "It has become part of the DNA of our retail stores." If you start with the ultimate question, it will influence your hiring decision. "You will begin with people who care about a customer's heart, not just their pocketbook," according to Johnson.

When Ron Johnson and Steve Jobs began bouncing around the idea of a retail store, there were no computer retailer stores to compare. They had all failed miserably. Remember that when Apple opened its first store, the iPod was still in development and the Macbook, iPhone, and iPad were years away. So to get people in the door, Apple had to rely on giving people an experience that would enrich their lives. The stores wouldn't just sell computers. They would inform, illuminate, and inspire. They would create such a delightful interchange between the employees and customers that the customers would hardly be able to contain their excitement and would spread the word. Apple customers would be its best sales force. Johnson embraced NPS to measure how successful Apple was creating customer advocates.

According to Reichheld, Apple Store employees know where they rank among their peers in terms of NPS and where their store ranks relative to other stores in the region. Promoters are celebrated.

Apple Store managers recognize employees who create promoters of their customers; some stores even put photos of these employees next to the promoter's comment text, and then scroll them across a large-screen TV monitor in the employee break room. Meanwhile, Apple's central NPS team analyzes customer feedback from all the stores to understand the systemic reasons for promoters' enthusiasm. Though you might expect that the primary source of enthusiasm was Apple's amazing products or its cool store design, by far the most common reason promoters give for their happiness is the way store employees treated them.[7]

The higher the NPS, the closer Apple employees are to reaching their goal of enriching lives.

Apple began measuring NPS in 2007 when there were 163 stores. The NPS score was 58. Today, with well over 350 stores, Apple's NPS score tops 70 percent and some of the best stores rank above 90 percent, a remarkable achievement. "Where a typical electronics store might record $1,200 per square foot in sales, mature Apple stores exceed an estimated $6,000 per square foot. This is by far the highest productivity in retailing of any kind."[8]

Johnson realized that only passionate employees who were promoters themselves could ever transform customers into promoters, and that's why feedback is so critical between employees and managers. Both must feel comfortable about bringing up issues that might impact the NPS ranking. Apple is so serious about internal promoters, it developed a Net Promoter for People (NPP) system. Under NPP, store employees are surveyed every four months to determine whether or not they would recommend the store as a great place to work. Yes, profits are important. But profits won't appear unless you first enrich lives, and that includes the lives of your employees.

Measuring Customer Feedback

A few minutes after I left an Apple Store having purchased a Macbook Air, I received an e-mail with the subject line: "Share your thoughts on the Apple Store." It explained that Apple would like my feedback to make my next visit even better. The e-mail said it would take five minutes to fill out the survey. The survey is facilitated by a third-party, independent market research firm, but the questions are all based on NPS.

The first two pages of the Apple feedback form asked simple questions to determine what type of product I had purchased and whether I bought it online or in the store. Page three is where it became interesting with the following questions:

"Overall, how satisfied were you with your most recent experience at the Apple Store?" The score reflected a 0 to 10 scale: 0 = Not at all satisfied, 5 = Neutral, and 10 = Extremely satisfied.

The next question was the ultimate question: "How likely are you to recommend the Apple Store to a friend or family member?" Again, 0 means "Not at all likely" and 10 means "Extremely likely."

Page four asked questions such as, "How did this particular visit influence your likelihood to recommend the Apple Store?" It also contained an open field where I could fill in my response to the following question: "What would you tell someone when recommending the experience at the Apple Store?"

The following question was intended to measure the elements Apple believes are important to the overall customer experience, "When thinking about your experience at the Apple Store, how would you rate your satisfaction with the following aspects?"

- Store employees were friendly and made me feel welcome.

- I was assisted in a reasonable amount of time.

- I was given the personal attention I wanted.

- Store employees were knowledgeable about products and services.

- The checkout process was efficient.

The final question is also meant to evaluate the efficacy of the feedback loop, "Which of the following benefits, if any, have you heard of at the Apple Store (select all that apply)?"

- Personalized setup of your new Apple product
- Free workshops, including hands-on classes
- Technical support and repair services at the Genius Bar
- One to One program
- A dedicated business team
- The Apple Store app for the iPhone[9]

Apple Store employees realize that each of these store elements improves the quality of the customer experience. They are trained to make sure the customer is aware of the classes, workshops, Apple Care support, and so on. It's drilled into them daily. If they read it or heard it once during their initial training, they would likely forget to bring them up. But since they are given feedback every day, they rarely miss an opportunity to educate the customer.

A Tale of Two Scores

In October 2011, Sheila Seberg of Newport Beach was forced to cancel a flight on US Airways because her husband had suffered a major heart attack. The airline refused to refund the value of the $560 ticket but would extend the time in which it could be redeemed, so long as Seberg paid a $150 fee to change it!

"I was shocked,"[10] Seberg told a newspaper. "It's not like I frivolously decided not to take the trip. My husband almost died. But they showed no compassion." The Sebergs were loyal customers. They had racked up frequent flyer miles because Seberg's husband, Richard, was a dentist and flew US Airways every week to Las Vegas, where he had a second practice. He flew every week for fifteen years.

I read the Seberg story in the *Los Angeles Times*. Seberg had become a detractor, and in these days of rapidly traveling social media, any negative comment gets a megaphone. Seberg posted a comment to a social network that, in turn, caught the eye of a reporter in Los Angeles. On Twitter the story got retweeted hundreds of times with added comments such as "Ahhh, just another example of US Airways glorious customer service (note sarcasm)," or "US Airways is the WORST. Read about MY experience with them...." People were not only reading and sharing Seberg's story, they were adding their own! On a whim, I checked the NPS ranking for US Airways. I thought I had discovered a typo when I read "negative 12 percent." That's right. US Airways had net more detractors than promoters. A negative NPS score can't be good for anyone—employees, customers, or shareholders.

During the same week Seberg's US Airways story was circulating on the Internet, another story was going viral. This story involved a ten-year-old girl who had saved her allowance money for nine months to buy a new product. She literally brought a mason jar full of coins and cash to the store, but it had just closed. When the little girl and her parents saw that it was closed, they were sad and decided to walk around the mall. Much to their surprise, a store manager caught up to them, apologized, and led the girl back into the store. The employees all applauded and made the little girl feel like a princess. She poured out the contents of her jar and bought her product. As she was leaving, an employee approached her and said, "I have to tell you. This made my day." This store had an NPS of more than 70 percent. It was an Apple Store, and the product was an iPod Touch. This story, too, hit the blogosphere and was retweeted hundreds of times.

Both stories reinforce the power of feedback, or the lack of it. It's likely that the US Airways employee didn't even know about NPS nor was given feedback by a manager on how to improve the customer experience. The employee was also not empowered to do what is right. Remember the admonition that Steve Jobs left to his employees shortly before his death: "Don't ask, what would Steve do? Instead ask, is it the right thing?"

By contrast, the Apple employee who chased after the girl's family and invited them back into the store knew three things: he would not be chastised for breaking the rules, he was enriching a little girl's life, and the parents would probably offer glowing feedback, which they did through their social networks.

"Every leader of a business leaves a legacy when he or she departs, and it is that legacy by which a leader is judged. If you want to leave a legacy that extends beyond profits, a legacy of caring about customers and employees and about the kind of company you have built, a legacy of enriching the lives you touched, NPS is an indispensable tool,"[11] says Reichheld. Anyone can sell products. Most do it badly because they don't care about leaving a legacy. They don't care about enriching lives. Steve Jobs cared about legacy. Jobs told Isaacson, "I hate it when people call themselves entrepreneurs when what they're really trying to do is launch a start-up and then sell or go public so they can cash in and move on. They're unwilling to do the work it takes to build a real company, which is the hardest work in business. That's how you really make a contribution and add to the legacy of those who went before. You build a company that will stand for something a generation or two from now."[12] If you want to build a brand that awes people and a company that lasts, you must hire the right people, create the right culture, and constantly provide feedback for that culture to survive.

CHECKOUT

1. **Create daily opportunities for feedback between you and your team.** Check your egos at the door. Everyone must feel comfortable and confident giving and taking feedback. Ask them to be "authentic," and they might surprise you with their input.

2. **Design opportunities to solicit feedback from your customers after the transaction takes place.** Apple doesn't ask for feedback on the sales floor. This can be as simple as an e-mail survey or a brief phone call. Above all, the most important question to ask is, "On a scale of 0 to 10, how likely is it that you will recommend our product/service/company?"

3. **Learn more about the importance of feedback and the NPS customer satisfaction score.** Read *The Ultimate Question* by Fred Reichheld.

CHAPTER 6

Develop Multitaskers

The employees act like servants
when they're really kings of
customer service.

—Carolyn DiPiero, Apple customer

Carolyn DiPiero, a retired schoolteacher living in Modesto, California, walked into an Apple Store in August 2011 and had such a magical experience she had to share it with me. DiPiero had never used a Mac, but after her first visit to an Apple Store, she was turned into a customer and an avid evangelist.

For fifteen years DiPiero had been sharing a PC at home with her husband, and she finally decided to get a laptop of her own. But the decision wasn't easy at first. Her kids were divided on the topic. DiPiero's daughter was a Mac user but her son, a PC user.

"Why should I buy a PC?"[1] DiPiero asked her son.

"Because it's less expensive than a Mac," he said.

"Why should I buy a Mac?" DiPiero asked her daughter.

"Because it doesn't get viruses," she said.

The virus logic caught DiPiero's attention. "I was definitely tired of cleaning viruses off our PC," DiPiero told me. "Finding someone to cure a computer virus is tougher than finding a doctor who takes Medicare."

The Apple Store at Modesto's Vintage Faire Mall is sandwiched between two boutiques, Coach and bebe. DiPiero always knew it was different because, well, it looked different. Gazing through the megasized floor-to-ceiling windows, DiPiero could see that the store looked clean and uncluttered, a far cry from the typical department store DiPiero would visit. The design was just the beginning of DiPiero's Apple experience. It would be one of the most unique shopping experiences of her life and ultimately convince her to become an Apple customer.

Upon entering the store, DiPiero looked for the cash register. All department stores have a cash register, she assumed. She didn't see any. Instead "Jeff" approached her, introduced himself, and asked how he could help. "Everyone looked involved, interested, and interesting," she said. "At department stores, you can't find a clerk to help you or to talk to. And if you do, the employees are talking to each other about their work schedule or other office-related issues. Also, most employees never make eye contact. The Apple Store was completely different."

A Teacher Takes a Lesson from Apple

A former elementary schoolteacher, DiPiero was used to surveying the room to keep an eye on how everyone was interacting. She noticed that the Apple employees were doing the same thing, an action she described as "multitasking." Although employees were taking care of several people at the same time, DiPiero felt as though she was getting personalized attention. "It reminded me of being a teacher," she said. "When a teacher has yard duty, they multitask. They scan the playground. You're looking at the whole picture. You see those kids clear across the yard? What's brewing over there? Should I be ready to step in? You can tell by a child's body language. It's a skill you learn as a teacher." DiPiero says she has never used the word *multitasking* to describe employees in any other retail environment, but it was clear that Apple employees were indeed juggling multiple customers while making each one feel important.

DiPiero acknowledged that her experience ultimately led to her decision to buy a Mac instead of a PC. She was so overjoyed she developed this APPLE acronym to describe her experience, which she sent me in an e-mail:

A is for *awesome*. The staff listens, directs, and instructs.

P is for *pristine*. The store has a clean, uncluttered appearance.

P is for *patience*. The helpful and friendly staff take their time with customers.

L is for *learned*. Employees know their stuff, and they educate customers, too.

E is for *energetic*. Employees survey, greet, and respond to customers as soon as they enter.

Developing multitaskers can bring your company to the next level. Don't make the mistake of believing that an employee who is good at putting out one fire after another is a good "multitasker." That's not multitasking. Too many people equate multitasking with juggling multiple projects. If you juggle five projects at the same time and they all turn out badly, then what good does it do you? The same applies to customer communication. If you're proud of yourself for handling three customers at the same time, but none

Customers experimenting with iPads. *Source: Getty Images*

of them are likely to recommend your service to others, then what good does it do your organization? You might have answered their questions, but you failed to turn them into promoters. True multitasking is accommodating three customers and making them all feel special.

The average Apple Store attracts more than 20,000 visitors a week. It's rare to find an empty store. I live in a midsized town where few stores are ever really, really busy. It's the kind of place where there's always easy parking at the shopping mall, even during the holidays. I had to buy some accessories at the Apple Store one day, and because I just wanted to get in and out quickly, I decided to go on a Wednesday morning right when it opened, thinking that the store would be nearly empty with the exception of a few employees. I got to the store five minutes after the store opened at 10:00 a.m., and much to my surprise, there were fifty customers already there. *Fifty!*

The Apple Store is always busy. Always. Yet, I'm regularly amazed at the way Apple employees can carry on conversations with several customers and make everyone feel as though they are getting personalized attention. Does it happen each and every time? No, it doesn't. And when customers feel neglected, they are quick to voice their displeasure on Facebook or Twitter. It doesn't happen in every conversation, because multitasking is a very difficult skill to teach and to master. Apple simply cannot train 30,000 employees to master the skill of multitasking. But Apple employees get it right much more often than they get it wrong, and that's one of the reasons why Apple has far more "promoters" than it does "detractors."

Three's Not a Crowd

Our community manager, Carolyn, once returned to the office after spending an hour at a nearby T-Mobile wireless store. She didn't go to buy anything or to browse. She simply had one small question. As Carolyn entered the store, she was sure she would be done in minutes because there were only three people in the entire store. The trouble was there were only three employees, and nobody knew the first thing about multitasking. None of the employees made eye contact with her nor did they acknowledge her. Carolyn waited forty-five minutes, got her question answered, but left with such a bad taste for the experience that she left the service.

Compare Carolyn's experience to the day I walked into an Apple Store to purchase a MacBook Air. A Specialist patiently explained my options and answered my questions for nearly one hour (truthfully, I had made up my mind after ten minutes, but I wanted to see just how far I could push the customer experience). Now let's be honest. It's not reasonable to expect any Apple employee to spend one hour with one customer when dozens of others are looking for guidance. So they don't. They multitask instead. I felt as though the Specialist gave me her full and undivided attention when, in reality, she also made two other customers feel exactly the same during the time she was working with me. I spoke to the other two customers before they left the store. Both said they would give their experience a *10* on the Apple Store survey. Here's how we are all made to feel cared for.

Specialist: Carmine (she used my first name several times in the conversation), based on what you've told me, I believe the thirteen-inch MacBook Air with 128 GB of storage would best suit your needs. But it sounds as though you're still trying to decide between the thirteen-inch and the eleven-inch model. Take your time, try out each one, and I'll be here to answer any questions. Would you mind if I briefly help this person next to us while you're thinking about it?

Carmine: No, of course not. Go ahead. (By this time the Specialist had already built trust. I trusted that she was knowledgeable, helpful, and friendly. She also asked permission before interrupting the conversation.)

Specialist (addressing Customer 2)**:** Hi, welcome to the Apple Store. Are you interested in our notebook computers?

Customer 2: Yes, I am. Do these all come with the new operating system, Lion?

Specialist: Yes, Lion is installed on our computers. It's an awesome experience. I think you'll be really pleased. As you can see, we are very busy today. I'd love to help you right after this customer, but you might be served more quickly if you request a Specialist using the iPad next to the computer. Just tap "ask for Specialist," and someone will be right over.

Customer 2: OK. I'll do that. Thanks.

Specialist: No problem. I'll come back to check on you. (The Specialist now "owns" the relationship. You will learn more about owning the customer relationship in Part II.)

Specialist (turning back toward me): I see you're holding the eleven-inch MacBook Air. Can you believe how thin and light it is? Pretty cool, isn't it?

Carmine: It is. But I think the screen is too small for me. I like the thirteen-inch model better.

Specialist: I can see why you would like it. It sounds like you're on the road a lot and you're not always plugged in to a larger display. (The Specialist repeatedly referred to our previous conversation, demonstrating that she did, indeed, listen to me.)

By this point in the conversation, another Specialist, "Sam," had arrived to help Customer 2. But while we were discussing my decision, a third customer interrupted our conversation. Interruptions occur frequently at the Apple Store, and although some customers can be rude, Apple employees treat everyone with a smile and a friendly greeting. If the employees are irritated, they don't show it. I'll continue with my observations:

Customer 3: Excuse me. I just came in to buy these headphones. Where can I go to ring it up?

Specialist: I can help you here and get you on your way. I just need your credit card. (Apple employees carry EasyPay devices, specialized mobile checkout systems.)

Specialist (turning toward me as Customer 3 is fumbling for credit card): Have you decided between the 128 GB or the 256 GB model?

Carmine: Well, despite all of the multimedia currently on my computer, it still only takes up 75 GB on my hard drive. So I think I'll be OK with

128 GB of storage. (Although the Specialist is handling another transaction, she is maintaining eye contact with me and nodding in agreement. She is still actively engaged in the primary conversation.)

Customer 3: Well, that was easy. Thanks.

Specialist: No problem. Thanks for coming in. We'll see you next time. (Apple employees end conversations with an invitation to continue the relationship, which we will discuss more in Part II.)

Specialist: Carmine, it sounds like you've made up your mind. I think you'll be very happy. I can't wait to hear about your experience. Before you leave, I'll give you my card so you can contact me with any questions. (By giving a customer a card with a name and number on it and inviting the customer to extend the relationship, employees can turn someone from a "satisfied" customer into a "promoter.")

Let's return to the example of the ice cream parlor to see how the Apple experience translates into another, non-computer-related field. Here are two scenarios of how a customer interaction might play out. The first is conducted by a typical, nonmultitasking employee juggling multiple customers. The second scenario is an example of effective multitasking.

Scenario 1: Ice Cream Parlor

Employee: Have you made up your mind?

Customer: No, I haven't.

Employee: OK, I'll take care of the next customer while you're thinking.

Scenario 2: Ice Cream Parlor

Employee: Have you chosen the flavor of ice cream you'd like to enjoy today?

Customer: No, I haven't.

Employee: Do you like chocolate, vanilla, or strawberry?

Customer: Oh, chocolate. I love chocolate.

Employee: So do I! Our flavor of the month is dark chocolate brownie. It's the richest chocolate in the store, and it's loaded with real brownie chunks. Please take your time, and I'll assist the next customer in line while you're deciding.

In *Customer Experience*, researchers discovered the customer emotions that drive or destroy value. Emotions that destroy value are irritation, hurriedness, neglect, and frustration. Emotions that build value are trust, happiness, pleased state, and care.[2] Multitasking leaves everyone feeling as though they have been acknowledged, served, and cared for. That helps build trust, happiness, and pleasure. It's the Apple way.

> *The Apple Store is insanely awesome. You leave the place happy.*
> —Carlos B.

Master Multitasking in Three Steps

My wife, Vanessa Gallo, manages our practice, Gallo Communications Group, where we provide communication skills coaching to some of the world's most admired brands. She has a master's degree in developmental psychology and worked as an instructor at San Francisco State University as well as a corporate trainer for a large, publicly traded company for years before her role at Gallo Communications. Vanessa applies psychology to all facets of communication and customer service, including the art of multitasking.

Early in Vanessa's career, she also managed a tasting room for the largest winery in northern California's Livermore Valley. If you've ever been to a very busy winery, then you know it requires the best multitasking skills an employee has to offer. At any given time there could be dozens of people in the room, some who are enjoying their wine while the staff provides education on each glass. Staff must move from person to person, provide insight, and keep track of where the person is in the tasting process, in addition to closing transactions at the register upon checkouts. Additional patrons are behind the first row of people already at the bar. They are waiting or trying to find room to squeeze in. Meanwhile, an entire tour bus of visitors could show up pouring fifty people through the door. When I visited Vanessa, I had two thoughts. The first: I would never want this job! The second: Everyone in the room was calm, perfectly choreographed, and the customers were enjoying a memorable experience.

When I asked Vanessa about why effective multitasking is so important when handling a packed house, she gave me an interesting way to look at it. When you invite people to your home for a party, the hospitable routine should include greeting your guests upon arrival, directing them where to put their coats, showing them where the drinks and goodies are, introducing them to other guests who've already arrived, and possibly giving them a tour. This routine requires a host who can multitask and do so in a way that makes the guests feel welcomed and content, which ultimately leads to a successful party.

Customer service associates need to put on their party hats and treat their next busy shifts like they are hosting a get-together in their home, to ensure their customers feel welcomed and satisfied when they leave. More times than not, though, associates freeze up when too many customers show up at the same time. The common response is no response. Vanessa recalled a recent visit to a large home improvement store where she stood with an inquiring expression near an associate who was talking with another customer for more than ten minutes before he acknowledged that she was waiting for help! (She would have sought another associate for help had there been one around.) Would you wait ten minutes to greet one of your party arrivals? Not if you're a good host.

Three Steps to a Happier Customer

Some people are simply better at multitasking than others, but it is a skill that can be acquired and, in the real world, employers may not have the luxury to screen for customer service reps who are multitasking superstars. In her role as a tasting room manager, Vanessa quickly learned that if her employees were skilled at multitasking, customer satisfaction would rise, sales would go up, and bonuses would be bigger! Needless to say, it didn't take the tasting room team long to buy in. The system that Vanessa developed, based on fundamental psychological principles of human behavior, is similar to the Apple experience described earlier. Her three-step process that helped the tasting room's sales soar is very simple. Rookies can adopt and use it to be more effective multitaskers when servicing more than one customer at a time: address, assess, assign.[3]

Step One: Address

This first step is the most important. When customers see the room is filled with other customers and there are only a few customer service reps to service them all, they are patient and understanding *only* when the rep acknowledges their existence. If you are waiting on someone when a new customer arrives, you should stop within ten seconds (if possible) of their arrival to do three things: (1) smile, (2) lock eyes, and (3) verbally welcome this new customer.

Eye contact is critical. Remember when we discussed friendly and fearless employees? Unfriendly and timid employees do not make eye contact. A 2008 study in Seattle found that bank robberies declined when tellers were taught to provide better customer service.[4] The program was called SafeCatch and taught employees to unnerve would-be bank robbers with eye contact, a smile, and a friendly greeting. Since bank robbers want to remain anonymous, they would leave the bank. I guess this is one case where turning off customers with a smile is a good thing!

An acceptable verbal remark to say to customers upon greeting them would be, "Thank you for coming in, I'll be with you shortly." An even better remark would be, "Thank you for coming in. I will be happy to help you today. Do you know what you are looking for?" This is a better response because it will give you more information to help you decide how quickly you can get to this person and determine what he or she needs. I recall a recent visit to a local large department store where I waited in line forever behind a customer who was arguing over a price on a sale item. The sales rep told me, "I'll be right with you," but all I needed to do was put something on hold so I could retrieve my wallet from the car. If she had said, "What do you need help with?" she would have learned that I didn't need much but for her to take my garment and put it aside. She could have done this easily while still dealing with the price whiner.

Step Two: Assess

Now that you know what the customer needs, this is where step two comes in—assess the situation and determine the best strategy for keeping this customer content while you continue to help your existing customer. You should be able to identify one of four plans to execute:

1. **Quick fix.** The need is a quick fix you can facilitate while still working with your existing customer (e.g., direct the customer to where she needs to go, hand him a menu, give her directions). If you go with this option, be sure to tell your existing customer something like this, "It's important that I continue to help you, so please hold on one moment while I get this other customer on track."

2. **Kill two birds.** If the new customer has the same need as the one you are currently serving, bring them together and help them at the same time. Here's an example from Vanessa's tasting room experience: when an existing customer would want to taste the same flight of wines as another customer who just walked in, Vanessa would set them up with glasses and educate them about the wines in their flight at the same time. They appreciated that she made an effort to help them both in a timely manner, and the experience was more enriching with additional people involved.

3. **Enforce help.** The need is not a quick fix, and there is another rep close by who is available to help. Don't operate in a vacuum, or assume you have to take it all on. Use your teammates when possible, and doing so will foster a receptive and pleasant environment for your "guests" to wait in and for you and your team to work in.

4. **Monitor wait time.** If the need is not a quick fix and there is no one else around you can delegate to, then tell the new customer

to hang on while you finish helping your existing customer. Be sure to check in regularly with the waiting customer.

The Specialist at the Apple Store who helped me with my MacBook Air purchase was not the first person who greeted me. She was assigned by the greeter because she worked at the Mac-Book table. When a second customer was also looking for service, my Specialist did not assign it to herself. She assigned the role to another Specialist. Only when the third customer approached us did my Specialist assign the task to herself because she knew she could handle it quickly. All the Specialists I encountered that day demonstrated this second but crucial step of the process brilliantly and smoothly.

Step Three: Assign

The final step in this multitasking process is to execute (or assign) the plan you've identified as the best choice during your assessment. If a monitored wait time is indeed the best plan, then make the wait bearable for the customer. Offer a glass of water, a brochure, a seat to sit in, or whatever is relevant in your space and industry. Check in with your waiting customer every minute. Phrases like, "Thanks for waiting," "I'm almost ready," "Can I do anything while you wait?" are all acceptable check-in statements.

Effective multitasking is like playing chess. You won't win the game if you focus only on each play at a time instead of strategizing what could happen if you make one move over another. Keep your eyes and mind open to the whole landscape. Anticipate and evolve your moves and strategy based on what is happening as well as what could happen. Addressing, assessing, and assigning a plan of action should take only less than a minute once you put it to practice, and when you do it successfully, your customers will love you for it. Make your customers—your guests—feel welcomed, entertained, and special, and never make them feel like they are unwanted. In return, you'll win their hearts. They'll roll with it because they get that a good host has to work the room, and you'll feel confident and empowered in your customer service role.

CHECKOUT

1. **Follow the three steps to a happier customer.** Train your employees to follow the three steps of effective multitasking: address, assess, and assign.

2. **Designate role models.** If you already have a person on your staff who is a great multitasker, you have a team leader whom other staff can observe during customer interactions as part of their training.

3. **Greet within ten seconds.** Regardless of how many customers are in your store or location, do not let more than ten seconds go by before acknowledging the presence of a new customer who walks in. Brands that stand out in customer service have learned that customers want to be acknowledged within ten seconds of entering a store, even if they cannot be served right away.

CHAPTER 7

Empower Your Employees

Intrinsic motivation is conducive to creativity.

—Daniel H. Pink

An Apple customer in Cardiff, Wales, Anna, once posted this Tweet to her three hundred friends: "Blown away by Apple customer service. Brand-new replacement iPad despite no insurance and the cracked screen being entirely my fault." Anna's experience is not unique. It happens quite often. It's not secret inside information. Anyone who monitors Twitter can see it.

On the same day that Anna posted her experience, "Rob" tweeted, "My mom dropped her iPhone in water, fried the hardware, and the Apple Store gave her a brand new one on the spot." When a customer buys an iPhone at the Apple Store, the device comes with a limited one-year warranty. It covers stuff that's Apple's fault—like defects in materials—and doesn't cover the stuff that's your fault—like "cosmetic damage'" (broken glass, dents) or damage caused by "accidents" or "liquid contact." In other words, if you drop your new iPhone in the toilet, you're out of luck, and Siri, the iPhone 4S personal assistant, can't help you. So how could Anna and Rob's mom get their devices replaced? The answer will tell you everything you need to know about attracting, retaining, and motivating A-players, people at the top of their game.

The Right Thing to Do

Apple employees are not supposed to replace devices that have been accidentally dropped, dunked in water, or otherwise damaged due to the customer's negligence. But sometimes they will replace devices that were dropped, dunked, and damaged if it's *the right thing to do*. Apple employees are empowered to make the right decision, and sometimes replacing a computer or iPod that's out of warranty is the most appropriate response. However, by the time you read this, I believe that this policy will be so well known that it wouldn't surprise me if Apple has to become more selective with its replacement units.

Fixing Relationships, Not Computers

Warranties are written in black and white, but Apple employees are empowered to make decisions in the gray area. They are trusted to make the right decision for the company and for the long-term relationship with a customer. If a customer brings in an iPhone that was accidentally dropped in a puddle, an employee at the Genius Bar might look up the customer's history, and if he feels that replacing the device will restore the customer's trust in the company, he will do so. The Genius's role is not to fix computers. It's to rebuild relationships. In the first ten years of the Apple Store, the company learned "a visit to the Genius Bar can fix more than computers; it can restore a customer's relationship with Apple."[1]

Compare this philosophy to other retailers. A friend who works as an assistant manager at a department store says she is "empowered" to give a customer a $20 gift card if the company messed up in some way. At least that's what employees are told. The truth is harder to come by. The department store's employees must get multiple levels of permission, all the way up to district manager. Since my friend's district manager takes days to respond to a phone call or e-mail, she knows that offering a $20 gift certificate is fruitless. So she doesn't.

Now don't expect to just walk into an Apple Store and get your broken device replaced because you read it in this book. Remember, Apple hires "fearless" employees. If you show up and demand a replacement because you heard that someone else had a device replaced, an employee will probably remind you about the warranty and what it covers. Apple employees treat customers with respect, but fearless employees command respect in return. Now you know what's behind a Tweet such as this one: "Apple Store responded to my screen-shattered, out-of-warranty iPhone 4 by handing me a new one. Customer service so high it's embarrassing." Empower your employees to embarrass themselves every now and then.

> *I love how reasonable Apple is. They have strict policies, but they know how to make good exceptions.* —Joel K.

The Engagement Crisis

Empowered employees have higher levels of "engagement," meaning they are emotionally connected to their jobs and dedicated to providing the highest customer service. But as we've discussed, most employees are uninspired and disengaged. Less-engaged employees are more likely to leave an organization, leading to rising turnover costs, lower productivity, and growing disruptions.[2] I'm not sure how companies with disengaged employees can even stay in business. They will certainly never offer Apple-style customer service. Commentators praise Apple's success in retail by citing foot traffic, design, products, or the patented circular glass staircase. All of these items are important, but Apple's success begins with empowered and engaged employees who truly believe they are changing the world. If you don't get your internal customer right, you'll never do right for the customer.

Unmasking The Ritz-Carlton Mystique

You'll recall from Chapter 2 that before hiring an employee some Apple managers ask themselves, "Could this person go toe-to-toe with Steve Jobs?" The second question they ask themselves is, "Can this person provide Ritz-Carlton quality of customer service?" I've had the opportunity to interview The Ritz-Carlton leaders, and I learned that, like Apple, empowerment is one of the fundamental building blocks of The Ritz-Carlton experience.

For over two decades, "The Ritz-Carlton Basics" guided every interaction between employees and guests, and these twenty rules dictated everything, from exactly what to say (Never say "Hello." Use more formal greetings like "Good morning") to actions (Never let a guest carry his own luggage). But as the world changed, so did the typical Ritz-Carlton hotel guest, and it became time to rethink service values by empowering employees to think and act for themselves, but still in accordance with The Ritz-Carlton vision.

Senior leaders conducted dozens of internal focus groups, meeting personally with thousands of employees around the world to develop a new set of service values. Frontline employees were asking for more flexibility in the way they were allowed to interact with guests. They wanted to be "empowered" to do what they knew was right.

In a service environment like Apple or The Ritz-Carlton, the goal is to create an emotional engagement with the brand so strong that a Ritz guest will not consider staying anywhere else and an Apple customer would never consider buying a PC. At The Ritz-Carlton, the quality of the beds, furniture, or flat screen TVs are all part of the experience, but in a luxury hotel those things are expected. Once basic luxury standards are met, the emotional engagement comes through the experience guests have with employees. Nobody has an emotional experience with an object.

In 2006, The Ritz-Carlton introduced its new service values, guidelines for employees to follow during guest interactions. Among the values: "I am empowered to create unique, memorable, and personal experiences for our guests."[3] (Service Value 3); "I understand my role in creating The Ritz-Carlton mystique." (Service Value 4);

"I own and immediately resolve guest problems." (Service Value 6); and "I am involved in the planning of the work that affects me." (Service Value 9). *I am involved.* These three words hold the key: invite your employees to participate in the creation of the brand, listen to what they have to say, act on their feedback, and they will walk through walls for you.

The Ritz-Carlton "Wow" Stories

Every day at the nearly a hundred Ritz-Carlton hotels around the world, in each department, on every shift, employees are called in for a "lineup," a staff meeting. The lineup is a fifteen-minute pep talk where wow stories are shared with everyone on the team. Wow stories feature The Ritz-Carlton hotel employees who create unique, memorable, and personal experiences for guests. A housekeeper who shows up for the evening shift in Shanghai will hear the same story as a doorman had heard in Hong Kong an hour earlier or a waiter in New York the next morning. In my book *Fire Them Up!*, I included some real wow stories. Here's one example:

> Today's wow story is from The Ritz-Carlton, San Juan Hotel, Spa & Casino and demonstrates today's "Service Value 1 in building strong relationships to create Ritz-Carlton guests for life.
>
> A married couple had been repeat guests at the hotel for the past few years. This year, a suit the wife was wearing was stained due to a spill on the counter. It was a very expensive suit and it was sent immediately to the laundry to be dry-cleaned. The stain, however, would not come out. The guest was very disappointed when she checked out, as nothing could be done to restore her ruined suit. Harold Rodriquez, Laundry Supervisor, called her home to apologize and asked if she was willing to FedEx her suit so that another attempt could be made to remove the stain from the suit. The guest agreed and Harold contacted an external laundry company for their assistance. Harold called the guest every day to keep her informed on the progress of the suit cleaning. Unfortunately, the outside laundry company was unable to remove the stain.

Harold wanted to turn the situation around and build a relationship for life with the guests. He therefore proceeded to get the cost of the suit reimbursed, took the check, got on a plane to New York, drove to their home, and rang the doorbell. When he introduced himself, the couple looked surprised. Harold received smiles and hugs. Their gratitude was priceless. He had created a memorable experience for the guests by turning a problem into an opportunity to "wow" them with genuine care and service excellence. His belief that nothing is impossible: when you do something from the heart everything in life can be accomplished.[4]

If you find this story hard to believe, rest assured, it is true. The hotel employees, the "ladies and gentlemen" of The Ritz-Carlton, are empowered to do what's in the best interest of the guest and what they believe is required to nurture a long-term relationship between the guest and the brand.

Drive

In *Drive*, Daniel Pink analyzed dozens of studies in the area of human motivation. Pink believes that most businesses fail to understand what motivates people. "Too many organizations still operate from assumptions about human potential and individual performance that are outdated, unexamined, and rooted more in folklore than in science."[5] Companies that pursue outdated methods of motivation are quick to create pay-for-performance incentives like commissions or free gifts to get employees to work harder. Yes, people have to earn a living. Wages, salaries, and benefits are what Pink calls "baseline rewards." If those baseline rewards are not adequate, then employees will focus on the unfairness of the situation instead of delivering exceptional customer service. "But once we're past that threshold, carrots and sticks can achieve precisely the *opposite* of the intended aims,"[6] writes Pink. Carrots and sticks can extinguish motivation, diminish performance, crush creativity, encourage shortcuts and unethical behavior, and foster short-term thinking.

Pink discovered that for routine tasks that do not require a lot of creative thinking, external rewards can provide a small motivational boost. But for higher thinking creative tasks, the best approach is to motivate employees with a combination of praise, positive feedback, and the feeling of autonomy and empowerment.

Returning to Apple, store Specialists are paid an average of $11.25 an hour. The salary ranges from $9 to $16 an hour, comparable to wages at other retailers. The technicians who operate the Genius Bar can make anywhere from $32,000 to $50,000 a year, the equivalent salary for an assistant or store manager in another noncomputer retail store. This salary range meets Pink's criteria of a baseline reward. So how then do you explain the fact that Apple employees are passionate, friendly, and motivated to create a superior customer experience? Intrinsic motivators make the difference.

Purpose and Praise

An analysis of intrinsic employee motivation wouldn't be complete without examining the importance of the twin pillars of purpose and praise. Pink says that Motivation 2.0 centered on maximizing profits. Motivation 3.0 seeks to reclaim an aspect of the human condition that most corporations have overlooked: the emotional catalyst of working for a grander purpose beyond just making money. Pink quotes former McDonald's executive Mats Lederhausen who says, "I believe wholeheartedly that a new form of capitalism is emerging. More stakeholders (customers, employees, shareholders, and the larger community) want their businesses to have a purpose bigger than their paycheck."[7]

The feeling of purpose relates to the discussion of vision in Chapter 1. Vision attracts evangelists. Steve Wozniak was wooed by Jobs's vision to put a computer in the hands of everyday people. People want to know that their work is adding up to something great. Steve Jobs once said, "Being the richest man in the cemetery didn't matter to me. Going to be bed at night saying, 'We've done something wonderful,' that's what matters."

Instill your employees with a sense of purpose beyond making money. Google specifically states that monetary incentives are "secondary to career growth, work environment, and engaging work opportunities." By focusing on these qualities Google seeks to develop motivated and collaborative employees who pursue achievements not for the money but for the sake of innovation, progress, and accomplishment. One offshoot of the Google philosophy is its well-known policy of giving engineers 20 percent time: one day a week when employees can work on any project of their choosing even if it has nothing to do with their day-to-day assignments. The social media site LinkedIn has a similar program. I was invited to speak about communication skills, and it was open to any employee who wanted to attend. The presentation was held on a Friday, and I noticed other speakers as well, representing a wide variety of interests, including a yoga instructor. On one Friday a month, the company devoted the day to personal growth and learning. Employees were even encouraged to shadow peers in other departments who perform different functions. The more you show that you care, the harder employees will work for you and the more creative they will be in moving your brand forward.

I had the opportunity to speak with Google's vice president Marissa Mayer. She told me that one of the keys to motivating young people especially is to give them a sense of empowerment and purpose. She said that employees want more than a paycheck. They want to feel as though they are contributing to the growth of the company. Mayer holds office hours each day to help people feel that sense of purpose. Office hours begin at 4:00 p.m. each day and last for about ninety minutes. Employees add their name to a board outside her office, and she gives them about fifteen minutes of time. Sometimes project managers need approval on a marketing campaign or just a few minutes to pitch their idea. According to Mayer, many of Google's most interesting projects got their start during office hours. It gives employees a voice. They are heard, and sometimes that's all they're looking for.

Zappos is another company considered the gold standard when it comes to customer service. When I visited Zappos headquarters in Henderson, Nevada, I was hit with a wave of fun, enthusiasm, and employee engagement the likes of which I've rarely seen in corporate America. Trust and empowerment is the name of the game.

Every employee I met was happy—really happy. It starts during the hiring process. Zappos CEO Tony Hsieh told me that one of the questions he asks of new recruits is, "On a scale of 1 to 10, how weird are you?" Someone who answers *1* might be too uptight for the Zappos culture. Someone who answers *10* might be too nutty!

Just as Walt Disney believed every cast member should reflect the brand, so too do Zappos employees reinforce the brand's culture. My first taste of the culture started with the driver who picked me up from my hotel. The driver said she shared time as one of the receptionists. When I asked why she picked me up when I could have taken a cab, she said, "We do this for all our guests. We treat you as family. If your family is in town, you'd pick them up, wouldn't you?" I was beginning to understand how Zappos grew from a start-up in Tony Hsieh's apartment to a billion-dollar-a-year customer service champion. During the Zappos tour I noticed the office of the Zappos "goal coach."

"What's a goal coach?" I asked a lady sitting in the office.

"We help people reach their goals," she responded.

"Oh, you mean teach them leadership skills or other skills related to their work?"

"Leadership is part of it, but we literally help people achieve their dreams, regardless of whether those aspirations are work-related or not. For example, one person came in this week and wanted to learn to play guitar. So we helped him find lessons. Another woman was procrastinating on the book that she wants to write, so we sat down and developed a schedule together."

"What does that have to do with Zappos?" I asked.

"It has everything to do with Zappos," she said.

Tony Hsieh will tell you that Zappos is not in the business of selling shoes. It's in the business of delivering happiness—to customers and to employees. Happy employees equal happy customers, and happy customers equal big profits. It's a simple equation that works for Zappos. It works for Apple. It will work for you, too.

In Apple Store heaven this morning. For unfortunate circumstances, but it's still heaven! —Marie D.

When Doubts Diminish and Spirits Soar

When people receive genuine praise, their doubts diminish and their spirits soar. Apple employees who make a mistake are not reprimanded harshly in front of their peers. They are simply pulled aside, asked to try harder the next time, given a high five, and put back on the floor. When they do well, they are often praised in front of their peers.

Sometimes praise comes in the form of encouragement when a person messes up. Years before former GE CEO Jack Welch earned the nickname "Neutron Jack," he almost blew up a factory for real. In 1963, early in his career, Welch was sitting in his Pittsburgh office when he heard a tremendous explosion outside. The blast blew the roof off the factory across the road. Nobody was seriously injured, but Welch admitted it was entirely his fault and drove a hundred miles to explain the incident to a corporate group executive. Welch figured he would be fired. Instead his boss was more concerned that Welch had learned something from the accident to prevent something like it from happening at his factory or any other factory, for that matter. "When people make mistakes, the last thing they need is discipline. It's time for encouragement and confidence building,"[8] Welch said.

Stephen J. Dubner, coauthor of *Freakonomics*, cautions, "One mistake a lot of people make when creating incentive schemes is thinking that financial incentives are the most powerful incentives going. In fact, social and moral incentives are often more powerful. The other thing to consider is what I sometimes call 'local fame'; very few of us want to be (or will ever be) truly famous. What we want is to be famous 'locally,' if even for a short time—that is, known well among our peers, families, friends, etc., for having done something well and noteworthy."[9]

Remember The Ritz-Carlton wow stories? Those stories are told at staff meetings so the person who played an important role in creating the customer experience is praised in front of his or her peers. Praising an individual publicly serves two purposes: it reinforces behavior the organization is attempting to replicate, and it gives the person "local fame" among peers. Praise and local fame touches people emotionally.

At Disney theme parks, leaders carry cards they use to provide instant recognition to employees who go above and beyond what is expected when serving a guest. On one half of the card, the leader describes the employee's conduct and hands it to the cast member, an action that is often enough to make the person's day. The leader keeps the other half of the card with the employee's name and turns it in for a prize drawing at the end of each month. The prizes, like iPods or movie tickets, are great, but it's the public recognition that cast members cherish. I recently heard about a school that gives "character counts" cards. The cards work in exactly the same way as the Disney cards, but instead of a supervisor handing out the cards to employees, teachers hand out the cards to students. A drawing is held at the end of every month, but instead of material prizes, a student might win ice cream with the principal. This is a proven method to encourage the repetition of positive behavior and to give your employees (or students) a chance to shine in front of their peers.

Filling Emotional Tanks

Jim Thompson is the executive director of the Positive Coaching Alliance, a nonprofit organization that has sparked a movement of 200,000 youth sports coaches, training in the group's mission: to use sports to teach character. Double-Goal coaches are those who want to win, but also aim to teach life lessons through sports. According to Thompson, there are an infinite number of teachable moments in youth sports that are overlooked by coaches and parents who are obsessed with winning. For example, if a kid strikes out, a First-Goal coach might have a conversation with the player about improving his mechanics. A Double-Goal coach covers the mechanics but also uses the moment to teach traits like resilience, bouncing back from setbacks, and giving it your best shot.

Effective praise is a key component of the Positive Coaching program. According to Thompson, the secret to effective praise is the "Magic 5:1 Ratio": find five reasons to praise for every one thing to criticize. Thompson calls it filling a person's emotional tank:

> We all have emotional tanks like a gas tank in a car. If it's empty, your car doesn't run. If it's low, you're not going to perform well. You can get people to do something out of fear for a short term. But the very best coaches build up their athletes or employees so they are excited and can't wait to go to work

and face the challenge. Constant criticism drains tanks. We're not anti-criticism, but you need to offer receivable criticism. I may be right in my criticism, but if I'm draining their tank while I'm doing it, they may spend internal emotional energy resisting, arguing, and not embracing the criticism. Give receivable feedback.[10]

According to Thompson, praise should be offered in what he terms a "criticism sandwich." For example, a young basketball player keeps missing three-point shots due to a lack of follow-through. A criticism sandwich would begin by praising something the player is doing right. For example, "I like the way you bend your knees, that's where you are getting your power."[11] The praise could be followed by a constructive criticism, intended to help the player improve in a specific area: "If you remember to follow through—do the gooseneck—you'll make more shots." This would then be followed up with more praise, like a sandwich: "I also like the way you keep your eye on the basket after you've thrown the ball." With this approach, the player gets three coaching tips, with the criticism surrounded by two praises. It fills the player's emotional tank and helps steer the focus on improving, not wallowing in frustration.

Thompson believes the average person feels underappreciated, and surveys of workplace morale agree. Most people work hard but do not feel acknowledged, leaving them demoralized and fed up. "But in an environment where people are noticed for good things—or even for taking their best shot if they fail—they're more likely to be fired up!" says Thompson. A great coach can turn an athlete with a lot of heart and a little skill into a standout. Michael Jordan didn't win a championship until Phil Jackson came along (who, by the way, is a proponent for the Positive Coaching program and serves as its national spokesperson) and helped Jordan become a champion (six times)! Jackson used the same technique to help the LA Lakers win five championships. He must have done something right. See yourself as a Double-Goal coach in your business relationships: Help your employees and colleagues master "the mechanics"—the nuts and bolts of their job—while encouraging them to reach their potential as champions in and out of the office. That's the Apple way.

Virgin Group founder Richard Branson might have put it best when he said, "My approach to being a good boss is not different from being a good father. If you lavish praise on people, people will flourish. If you criticize people, they will shrivel up." Building an empowered workforce means giving people permission to do what they believe is right for the customer. But it also means building their confidence and bringing out the best in them. You can build people up by sowing the seeds of encouragement. Recognize their greatness publicly and praise their accomplishments.

On September 5, 2005, Steve Jobs gave a stirring commencement speech to the graduating class of Stanford University. "Your time is limited, so don't waste it living someone else's life,"[12] he said. "Don't be trapped by dogma, which is living with the results of other people's thinking. Don't let the noise of others' opinions drown out your own inner voice. And most importantly, have the courage to follow your heart and intuition. They somehow already know what you truly want to become." Steve Jobs never placed limits on himself, and he certainly didn't tolerate anything but excellence in the people who worked for him. You might not be surrounded by A-players at all times, but everyone (B- and C-players as well) is capable of rising higher if they believe in you, the vision, and themselves. Be the voice that guides others. Believe in people, encourage their potential, and inspire them to live their best lives.

CHECKOUT

1. **Foster empowerment.** What can you do to give your employees more autonomy, authority, and flexibility when it comes to serving the customer? Even small measures of empowerment will lead to huge returns in employee engagement and customer satisfaction.

2. **Share your own wow moments.** Steal a page from The Ritz-Carlton playbook and start sharing wow stories of employees who exceeded customer expectations.

3. **Offer genuine praise.** Praise your employees each and every day. Make your positive comments as public as possible.

SERVING YOUR EXTERNAL CUSTOMER

Every time I come to the Apple Store they tell me I have beautiful eyes. That's good customer service right there!

—Brittany, Apple customer

Think back to a bad customer experience. If you're like most people, you will not have to think back that far. Bad customer service seems to be the norm these days. Brands like Apple that are hailed as customer service champs do things differently. It starts with inspirational leadership on the executive and management levels. Leaders who fail to inspire their teams and to clearly communicate their vision will never build companies that are admired for their superior customer experience. How can they? Employees who are discouraged, dejected, and demoralized have zero chance of engaging customers and making them feel good about their experience with the brand.

The first secret to offering insanely great customer service is to make sure your employees are happy, motivated, and passionate. But passion and energy take you only so far. Step two is to master the skills required to make your customers feel special. *What* you say and *how* you say it will make all the difference. In this section we begin with the Apple five steps of service that all employees are trained to follow in every customer interaction. These steps are so important that I urge you to study them and promptly call a meeting to share the steps with your coworkers and staff. For your brand to succeed in this hypercompetitive global economy, every person in the organization must internalize these steps and live these principles every day.

CHAPTER 8

Follow Apple's Five Steps of Service

You don't need to stock iPads to create an irresistible retail environment. You have to create a store that's more than a store to people.

—Ron Johnson

Walk into an Apple Retail Store, and you'll be greeted with a warm, friendly, cheery welcome within seconds of stepping inside. Approaching customers with a warm welcome is the first of five steps employees are instructed to take to create an enriching and memorable experience for Apple Store customers. All employees know the steps of service as the acronym *APPLE*:

Approach customers with a personalized, warm welcome.
Probe politely to understand all the customer's needs.
Present a solution for the customer to take home today.
Listen for and resolve any issues or concerns.
End with a fond farewell and an invitation to return.[1]

These five steps are taught to every Apple Retail Store employee. The steps are also practiced by other brands in a variety of industries as the foundation to delivering exceptional experiences. Some brands like AT&T retail stores adopted and modified the five steps with direct input from Steve Jobs. Other brands copy components of the steps with slight modifications. This five-step approach is a proven winner, and since Steve Jobs once said, "Good artists copy; great artists steal," let's steal a page from the Apple playbook and review the five steps of service in more detail.

The Apple Five Steps of Service

Step One: Approach Customers with a Personalized Warm Welcome

The key words in this first step are *approach, personalized,* and *warm.* Apple employees are empowered to interpret the greeting to fit their personality and to give the customer the type of attention the customer desires. Some customers just expect a smile as they walk toward the back of the store to buy new headphones, while others are there to buy a Mac for the first time and would like a deeper, more personalized and educational experience. The key is to make sure that customers are greeted by a friendly face that makes eye contact and is committed to creating a customized, unique, and meaningful experience *each and every time.*

Approaching customers with a warm welcome makes common sense, so it's baffling to find so few businesses that adopt this strategy. It's not that different from inviting someone to your house. When someone knocks on the door, do you simply open the door, walk away, and ignore that person? If so, please don't invite me to one of your parties! How would it make you feel to enter a home only to find your friend or the host of the event sitting on the couch watching television without smiling or even acknowledging your arrival? You would turn right around and leave, wouldn't you? It's rude, obnoxious, and borderline abusive. Yet most of us, as consumers, put up with this treatment all the time from retail stores and companies of all sizes. If you call a company and you rarely, if ever, get a live person on the line, then you are not receiving a warm welcome. If you leave a message or send an e-mail to someone at that company, and nobody calls you back or responds to your e-mail, you are not receiving a warm welcome. It's time to take your business somewhere else.

On Black Friday, 2011, I conducted an informal experiment at my local shopping mall. It was completely unscientific but very instructive. As you know, Black Friday is when merchants offer steep discounts to get people through the door to kick off the all-important holiday buying season. The crowds are enormous, and some people, like myself, purposely avoid venturing anywhere near a mall on that day. But when my family expressed an interest in going, I reluctantly decided to take the opportunity to conduct my little experiment despite the stressful crowds. Oh, what I'll do in the name of research!

When we arrived at the mall, I had three stores on my list to visit: Apple, AT&T, and LEGO. Each of these three retailers trains employees and sales staff to approach customers with a warm welcome. I wanted to see how well the employees of these brands follow their company's guidance on the busiest shopping day of the year. If employees greeted me upon entering the store in the middle of Black Friday madness, then I would know they had completely internalized the company's core customer service philosophy. Although the concept of greeting is intended for the customer service experience for these brands, it is widely known that greeting serves a double function, the second being shrinkage control, or the monitoring of theft. Retailers have noticed that greeting customers with a verbal welcome and making eye contact makes good business sense and deters people from leaving with goods that don't belong to them!

I first stopped at an AT&T retail store. We will discuss AT&T in more detail later in the chapter, but step one of its service philosophies is to make sure every customer is greeted within ten feet or ten seconds of entering the store. Well, it didn't take more than two seconds before "Brittany" welcomed me with a smile and a friendly, "Hello, welcome to AT&T." Although sixty to seventy people were in the store at the time, making it considerably busier than normal, I felt welcomed upon entering.

My second stop was the LEGO Store located directly next to the Apple Store that, not coincidentally, offers the same style of experience. Before I could even start my stopwatch to see how many minutes would go by, "John" greeted me, my daughters, and the friends who had accompanied us. "Welcome to LEGO. Let me know if you have any questions," he said. John then turned to a thirteen-year-old girl in our group who was wearing a holiday-themed snow hat and said, "I like your hat." A few minutes later the girl walked up to me and said, "Did you hear what he said? He likes my hat!" Amazing. That's all it took for this girl to feel special—a smile and a friendly "personalized" greeting.

The LEGO Store was packed. With about one hundred people in the store, there was hardly any place to stand, yet John was able to greet each and every person who walked through the door. When John had a break in between customers, I asked him why he said hello to everyone. "It's my job. I'm supposed to give everyone a warm welcome. It's part of our customer service experience," he said. I was stunned that John actually used the words "warm welcome." It seems as though this particular LEGO Store had learned something from the customer service champion next door.

Finally, we reached the moment I had been dreading: the Apple Store. I was dreading the event because Apple is busy on a slow day. Sure enough, it was slammed on Black Friday. I didn't even bother to count the customers, because I could not see past the first few feet. I saw only a wall of people. Yet each and every customer was being greeted with a warm welcome and a friendly smile. How could Apple welcome everyone? Instead of one greeter, *ten* people had been positioned at the front of the store. Instead of blue shirts, they were wearing red shirts to kick off the holiday shopping season and to stand out in the sea of customers. The warm welcome played such an important role in the Apple customer experience that it was never compromised, not even on the busiest shopping day of the year.

My experiment didn't end there. I had one more stop to test the theory that a warm welcome makes people feel special. Before we left the mall, I took my young daughters to a children's furniture store that does not have a stellar reputation for its customer interactions. The chain carries nicely built products, but it lacks the engaging exchange between customer and staff. We all walked in, I started my stopwatch, and we waited, and waited, and waited. Not one person approached us, even though several employees passed directly in front of us. I let my kids loose, and they seemed to have a good time pretend-playing with the faux kitchens and miniature houses that were set up. Yet no one took the opportunity to welcome us, provide information on the products, or make a sale. There were only fifteen customers in the entire store and five employees on the floor. I passed all five employees, and not one said as much as hello. Finally, after nine minutes "Lindsey" asked, "Are you finding everything OK?" I believe Lindsey addressed me only because I made eye contact with her. In other words, I gave her nonverbal permission to greet me. To top it off, the employees did not seem happy to be there either. It's no wonder there were only fifteen people in the store on such a busy day. Customers simply didn't feel welcome.

Approach with a warm welcome makes sense in nearly every conversation, off-line and online. For example, how quickly do you respond to customers who contact your company or comment on your product on Twitter or Facebook? For example, Pottery Barn, a division of Williams-Sonoma, requires its employees to answer the phone within three rings. A similar philosophy should be applied to your brand's digital touchpoints. One survey found that 70 percent of companies ignore customer complaints on Twitter.[2] This is a missed opportunity to deepen the brand's relationship with customers. In the same survey, 83 percent of the people who complained on Twitter said they "really liked" or "loved" getting a reply when the company did respond. When it comes to customer service, your customers want to be heard and they see social media as a direct and immediate way to engage with your brand. Most brands, however, ignore this channel and leave customers feeling even more frustrated.

How long should it take for a company to respond to a complaint or comment on Twitter? What is the digital equivalent to "ten steps or ten seconds?" Virgin America airlines is one brand that takes every opportunity on digital platforms to make customers feel welcome and special. It might not respond to Twitter comments in ten seconds, but it gets darn close.

Virgin America monitors Twitter posts and will often welcome travelers or address complaints within an hour. When I arrive at a Virgin America terminal, I'll check in on foursquare and share the post on Twitter. I've been surprised to receive a personalized welcome before I board the plane an hour or so later.

On December 6, 2011, Virgin America experienced a small customer service crisis as it upgraded to a new online reservation system. It had switched technology vendors, and the process was not going smoothly. Customers were furious. I found it interesting, though, that Virgin America was active on Twitter, apologizing and responding to complaints. The airline responded to complaints within an hour of the customer posting the Tweet. In total, the airline sent 12,000 Twitter replies in the days that followed the snafu. Here are some sample exchanges between Virgin America and its customers on Twitter (responses within the same hour as the original Tweet):

(Comment) @I_Heart_Romeo: Your competitors have functional reservation systems. Your system is infuriating.

(Response) @VirginAmerica: Apologies. Please know that this experience isn't typical. We're getting adjusted to a new res system. Thx 4 ur patience.

(Comment) @shyonelung: 28 minutes on hold with @virginamerica. What's over/under on someone answering within 40? Or whether I'll hang up before they do?

(Response) @VirginAmerica: Very sorry. We're sorting out a few bugs. Anything we can assist with? Pls follow & DM (direct message).

Virgin America also explained to some Twitter complainers that upgrading to a new reservation system is one of the most complicated things an airline can do and promised that it would be worked out in a matter of days. I was frankly shocked to see such a high level of customer service from any airline in the United States. But I was about to get an even bigger surprise. I decided to tweet a compliment to Virgin America and to request an interview for one of my articles (keep in mind that most PR folks on Twitter broadcast messages yet seldom respond to requests). Virgin America was different. Within 8 minutes—*8 minutes*—I received a direct message on Twitter from "Jill" in corporate communications with her e-mail address. We set up an interview for the next week. Virgin was modeling its commitment to being approachable and responsive.

> *Hanging at the happiest place on earth—the Apple Store!*
> —Melanie A.

Step Two: Probe Politely to Understand All the Customer's Needs

Most commissioned salespeople are interested only in getting you to buy something before you leave the store. It gets seriously annoying. I remember buying a nice shirt from a men's store, and when the salesman showed me a $100 tie, I asked him for something less expensive. He replied, "Oh c'mon, you can afford it. I have to feed my kids." Working on commission will make an employee do and say things that turn off instead of entice a customer. Would Apple prefer that you buy something every time you enter the store? Of course, it would. But Apple runs a noncommissioned sales floor, and employees are not pressured to make a sale. In fact, I've been told several times by Apple employees that they are not on commission. One Specialist said, "I'm not on commission. I'm here to help you grow." Since employees are encouraged to make you feel special, it means they must ask a lot of questions to find out what your needs are, enriching the overall experience.

Apple Retail employees "probe" in three ways: by asking open-ended questions, encouraging customers to have a meaningful dialogue, and contributing to the conversation. Here is how the first two steps of service might play out for a customer interested in, but not committed to, buying an iPad.

Employee: Hi, my name is Dave. Welcome to Apple. What brings you in today? (If a customer is clearly a business professional, a seasoned employee might open with a more formal greeting such as, "How can I best serve you today?")

Mom (Accompanied by daughter)**:** We're looking at iPads.

Employee: Awesome. Do you have any Apple products?

Mom: No, but my daughter has an iPod Touch.

Employee: That's a great start. A lot of the commands, navigation, look, and feel are the same as the iPad.

Employee (Turning to daughter)**:** Jane, do you have any questions before we get started? (The Specialist would have asked for names early in the conversation and would never ignore what Disney calls the "secondary customer," the person who can influence how the primary customer, in this case the mom, reflects on her experience.)

Jane: No.

Employee: OK, just let me know if you have any questions.

Employee (Turns to the mom and asks an open-ended question)**:** Betty, I'd like to take you on a tour of the iPad, but before I do, may I ask what you'll be using the iPad for? (Apple employees ask for permission before elevating the relationship.)

Mom: E-mail and photos, I guess.

Employee: Great. Photos are stunning on these new iPads. Would you mind if I took you on a quick tour of Photos?

In this conversation we see examples of a warm greeting, a combination of open and closed questions, as well as seeking permission to proceed with the next step in the sales process. Asking for permission seems to be a consistent theme in the Apple Store in all areas—sales, repair, and training. A customer might hear questions such as, "May I touch your computer?" "Would you like to see this feature?" or "Would you like to hear more about our classes?" Asking permission before probing gives the customer a sense of warmth, comfort, and trust. Probing lets the customer participate in the conversation and have a stake in her final decision. It creates a feeling of control. It validates the customer as a human being and not as a means to make a salesperson's numbers that day. It makes the customer feel like she's been heard and valued.

Step Three: Present a Solution for the Customer to Take Home Today

The culmination of this step can vary depending on the type of sale or interaction. For example, if a customer purchases a new product like an iMac, the employee will likely recommend a complete solution that includes the AppleCare Protection Plan and One to One training classes. In many sales environments the "extended warranty" is pushed on the consumer by eager salespeople who get a bonus or commission for selling those add-ons. What they don't tell you is that the rate of repair on digital cameras, flat screen televisions, or even vacuum cleaners for that matter is so low that extended warranties are hardly worth it. Another trick commissioned salespeople use, especially in the electronics industry, is to recommend expensive cables that are supposed to improve the quality of the sound or picture on the stereo or television. The salespeople can be very convincing. Who doesn't want a 24k gold-plated connector or a low-loss nitrogen dielectric? The cable sounds so impressive it must be good. But many experts say a $100 cable offers a nearly imperceptible improvement in quality over a $4 cable. Selling customers more expensive cables or a warranty they don't need does not qualify as a "complete solution." It counts as a salesperson enriching his pocket or satisfying company quotas, and not your life.

Why do most people hate the car-buying experience? It's because car salesmen are typically instructed to do whatever they can to get you into a car before you leave the lot. One Apple customer told me she walked into a store feeling sad and walked out happy, without buying a thing. Well, I've walked onto a car lot feeling happy and left feeling sad! The car-buying experience is simply not pleasurable for most people. On a noncommissioned floor like Apple where employees are trained to present a solution you can take home that day, it doesn't matter if you buy a product or not. You leave happy because you are presented with a solution. Let's return to the scenario where Betty was looking for an iPad.

Betty: You're right. Photos is wonderful. The pictures look incredible. But the iPad is a little more expensive that I thought, so I'll have to think about it. Thanks for your time.

Employee: Betty, we don't work on commission, so my only goal is to make sure you leave with all your questions answered so you can make an informed decision, whenever that may be. Betty, tell you what. We have free classes here at Apple. If you'd like, I can show you how to sign up on our website or I can sign you up right here. What you'll learn in one hour will blow your mind, and at least it will help you answer the question, "Is the iPad worth it for me?" I'd also encourage you to visit YouTube to see all the exciting things that people are doing with their iPads.

In this case, the employee told Betty that he is not on commission. Apple employees will not volunteer that information in every conversation, but they often will to make the customer feel more at ease. When I purchased my first MacBook, the Specialist who was helping me also reminded me that he wasn't on commission. I appreciated his honesty. It was very comforting and, yes, made me feel special and appreciated. Apple Specialists are perfectly content to let you leave the store without having made a purchase. They are more concerned about building a relationship for life. You might also note that the employee in the last scenario did not apologize for the price. In Apple's eyes, the best technology doesn't come cheap, but Apple also knows that people will pay a premium for exceptional customer service and technology that is simple, elegant, and easy to use.

Here's another example of presenting a solution the customer can take home today. I actually witnessed this conversation in an Apple Store when a customer complained about an iPhone that needed to be repaired, yet she could not get an appointment that day. The customer was demanding and somewhat rude, but the employee kept his cool and stuck to the five steps of service.

Employee: We can help you resolve the issue with your iPhone, but our Genius Bar is appointment driven and no techs are available to help you right now. I apologize, but we have no appointments left today. But ma'am, if you want someone to look at your iPhone today, there is another store that's fairly close. I can check to see if they have any openings today. If they do, can I make you an appointment for today?

Customer: No, that's not necessary.

Employee: Well, in that case, would you mind if we scheduled your next appointment together? We have an opening tomorrow morning, and I can get you in.

Customer: Sure, I'll take it.

In this scenario, the customer is still a little bitter, but we see the Apple employee taking the extra step to make sure the customer does not leave completely frustrated. The customer was presented with an alternative solution. She refused the solution to drive to another store the same day, but she did take the second choice for an appointment the following day. The customer came in grumpy because her iPhone was having problems and left reasonably happy, even though the problem had yet to be resolved.

The opposite scenario unfolds in restaurants every day. I cannot recall the last time a host or owner presented me with a solution I could take home today. When you call a restaurant that's fully booked for lunch or dinner, the typical response is, "I'm sorry we're fully booked tonight." That's it. No fond farewell, no solution, nothing. Here is what the experience at an Apple Store "restaurant" would be like.

Customer: Can I make a reservation for tonight, about 6:30? It would be for four people.

Host: I'm sorry. We're completely booked tonight. Have you been here before? (probe)

Customer: No, we haven't. That's why we wanted to try it.

Host: We would love to have you experience our restaurant. We have some new entrées on the menu that our diners are raving about. Can I help you find another date that would work?

Customer: Not now, thanks. I'm not sure of my schedule. I'm disappointed.

Host: Do me a favor. Please call us back when you're ready. Keep in mind that we tend to fill up on the weekend for both lunch and dinner. But if you make your reservation at least two days in advance, you should be fine. If you write my name down for reference, the next time you come in, we'll treat your table to a complimentary dessert of your choice. Our dessert chef was trained at one of the finest restaurants in New York, and a popular food critic said our baklava is the best he's ever had. I work here five nights a week, so just ask for me. But even if I'm not here, that dessert is on the house. We'll see you next time!

The host offered the diner a solution, gave the customer a reason to return (to redeem the dessert coupon and to try the critically acclaimed food), built rapport, and ended with step five—a fond farewell.

Step Four: Listen for and Resolve Any Issues or Concerns

Untrained and ineffective sales professionals in many industries are so focused on making the sale at all costs that they fail to actively listen. Apple employees are trained to acknowledge customers' questions, resolve their concerns, and help them understand all the benefits that come with the solution. In the previous scenario, the specialist asked Betty an open-ended question, listened to her response, and acted on Betty's remarks. Giving Betty a tour of Photos is the equivalent of a real estate agent letting the customer lead the tour of a house. A Realtor trained in the Apple experience would let a client walk through the house first, and instead of directing the tour, would ask, "What room is the most important to you?" If the response is "Actually, we're most interested in the backyard," the agent would suspend his predetermined tour of the house and start with the backyard. The agent has probed, listened, and responded.

You must understand that most people do not feel as though they are "heard" in their personal or professional lives. If spouses genuinely listened to each other, there would be no market for books such as *Men Are from Mars, Women Are from Venus*. If bosses really did read the comments in the suggestion box, there would be far fewer frustrated employees in the corporate world. When it comes to interpersonal communications, the number one lament is "my spouse (boss, friend, son, daughter) doesn't listen to me." By listening and truly acknowledging the needs of your customers, you can make your business an oasis of encouragement, empowerment, and excitement.

Step Five: End with a Fond Farewell and an Invitation to Return

Apple employees do not ask for direct feedback at the conclusion of the sales transaction. The feedback form is sent to customers once they leave the store. But it's clear that there is a direct correlation between how people feel when they leave and how likely they are to return or recommend the experience to someone else. When you leave someone's house, you expect to be sent off with a smile and an invitation to return, don't you? Imagine dropping in to a neighbor's house for a few minutes and as you leave, your neighbor says, "It's great to see you. Please bring the kids next time. We have some toys here that our grandkids love, and we know your children will like them, too." The farewell would make you feel special, wouldn't it? Believe it or not, this is not all that different from the fond farewell Apple Store employees are trained to deliver. When I purchased a MacBook, the Specialist who sold it to me ended with this remark: "It was great meeting you and learning more about the presentations you give. I think you'll be very happy with your MacBook Pro. Please come back for those One to One trainings, and if I'm here, I'd love to see what you created." It made me feel like she had taken a personal interest in my improvement.

The sales process at an Apple Store nearly always ends with congratulating the customer, summarizing some of the benefits of the purchase, and reinforcing the customer's decision to buy a particular product. Don't be surprised if the Apple Store employee escorts you to the door, especially if you have some large boxes, and says "thank you" and invites you to return. The employees at my local Wells Fargo branch in downtown Pleasanton, California, get up from their chairs and walk over to greet customers when they walk in. They also walk people to the door after every transaction. Some banks are closer, but I make it a point to go to this particular location for one reason only—it makes me feel good.

The fond farewell should take place regardless of whether or not the customer buys something. Remember, Apple is not in the business of moving boxes. It's in the business of enriching lives. That means if a customer leaves the store empty-handed but with a smile on her face, her life has been enriched and that's what matters. It would not be unusual to hear a farewell such as the following at an Apple Store:

> Tom, thanks for coming in today. I hope you have enough information to make your decision the next time you come in. And we hope you come back. We had a great conversation about college football, and you made my day. You know how hectic things get around here, and you gave me a chance to slow down and just be with a customer. Thanks for that. I'll see you next time.

In most organizations, especially retail, managers would jump all over an employee for spending too much time with a customer—either on the phone or in person. Former Apple Store employees have told me they never felt pressured to end a conversation. And this makes sense if the philosophy is to build relationships, not meet quotas.

Zappos, which receives consistently high marks for its extraordinary customer service, has the same Apple-like approach to the fond farewell. Zappos CEO Tony Hsieh once told me he heard about an employee who spent two hours on the phone with a customer. Instead of asking the employee why she had spent so much time on the phone, he simply asked if the customer was happy. Think about that question—was the customer happy? Hsieh did not ask, "Did you make a sale?" Hsieh is devoted to creating a culture that delivers happiness. Apple is devoted to "enriching lives," and so it would make sense for a manager to ask an employee who spent a long time with a customer, "Did you enrich that person's life today?"

> *Amazing customer service once again at the Church of Apple. Swapped cat pictures and stories with the sales guy.*
>
> —Bronwyn M.

It's not enough to train yourself—or your team—to deliver the five steps of service. You must help them understand *why* they're going through the steps. I've walked into several retail locations where a person is positioned to say hello to every customer. In one trip to my local mall I heard, "Hi, welcome to Justice" and "Hi, welcome to Pottery Barn." When I asked the employees in both locations why they greet each and every person who walks through the door, they both had exactly the same answer—I was told to do it. But when I asked someone in an Apple Retail Store why she greets people, she said, "We welcome our customers to enhance the overall customer experience. We're all about the experience. We want you to feel great about visiting our store, and we want you to have fun!" Clearly the Apple employee had internalized the brand's commitment to enhancing the customer experience.

What AT&T Retail Learned from Steve Jobs

The retailer who most closely—and successfully—follows the Apple model is, not surprisingly, the AT&T retail store. In fact, AT&T's customer service experience was directly influenced and inspired by Steve Jobs, who would call the company's head of retail to offer his advice. Of course, Steve being Steve, the advice was often unsolicited but always spot-on. Jobs had spent decades thinking about and refining the customer experience, and he could be very gracious in helping other brands—partners, especially—improve their experience.

Every month, millions of customers walk into an AT&T retail store to buy an iPhone, Android, or other phones that use the wireless carrier. AT&T's 2,300 retail stores have gone through significant changes in the past several years. Some are physical—less clutter, cool colors, tablet innovation walls, and much more. But the most important changes involve the way customers are treated and how its 26,000 employees communicate with those customers.

When the iPhone was first introduced in 2007, AT&T was inspired by Apple to raise the bar on the customer service experience. The company decided to differentiate itself around the experience. It was a smart strategic choice. As phone networks moved toward parity, retailers had two choices: to be the best price or have the best customer service in the industry. AT&T chose to focus on the customer.

AT&T developed a six-step process dubbed the AT&T Retail Experience.[3] The steps are remarkably similar to Apple's guiding principles. These tactics will work for any retailer or any service company seeking to improve the customer's experience with the brand.

1. **Greet and approach.** AT&T store employees now greet customers within ten feet and ten seconds of entering the door. I've challenged this tactic by entering several stores, and as I mentioned before, even on Black Friday. Employees never greeted me in ten seconds. They made it five seconds or less! AT&T retail staff will greet customers and introduce themselves by their first names. Once they know you on a first-name basis, they'll have started to make a deeper, more emotional connection with you.

2. **Build value.** An employee will ask customers specific questions to understand the purpose of their visit. This is consistent with the "Probing" step of the Apple experience. Every AT&T sales associate is certified in small business issues so they can address individual questions or questions specifically related to businesses. The purpose is to avoid a situation where several customers are waiting on one small business expert while other employees are free but unavailable to help.

3. **Offer solutions.** This is a key step. Employees are told that AT&T is not in the business of selling products. They are in the business of selling solutions. Customers don't walk through the door to buy a phone. They are interested in sending e-mail, texting, enjoying music, or sharing video with their kids. The wireless industry had always been considered a "transaction" oriented industry, but today's AT&T employees are much more focused on sending people home with the right solutions to help them lead more enriching lives.

4. **Gain agreement.** AT&T has a very low return rate, quite likely due to this critical fourth step. Employees must make sure they have helped customers walk out with the solutions they were

looking for. They are even taught to educate customers about solutions and benefits they were not aware even existed. This step cannot occur, however, unless the employee asks the right questions in the previous steps and develops a rapport with the customers.

5. **Walk out working.** This is the educational step. If a customer walked in wanting a phone to text her kids, the employee will show the customer how to take a photo and send it as an SMS. Employees will even set up a customer's e-mail in the store. Again, Apple does the same thing. Apple will transfer your data, set up e-mail, or do anything else you need to make sure your system works when you take it home. Reducing frustration after the sale raises the customer's perception of the overall experience.

6. **Thank and depart.** An AT&T employee will thank customers and walk them toward the door. Why? Because that's how you would treat guests in your home. As simple as it sounds, it rarely occurs in the retailing industry, with one notable exception—Apple.

Like Apple, AT&T expects every customer to walk out with a smile. Every employee in every store is expected to model the six behaviors, and if a salesperson cannot exhibit these behaviors in every interaction, there should be no role for that person at an AT&T store. The stores are very strict about the training and have high expectations for each and every one of AT&T's 26,000 employees.

Why Men Cheat and Why Brands Fail

As I was writing this chapter, I heard a radio interview on the topic of why men cheat. A marriage counselor was giving explanations for why men stray from their wedding vows. As I listened to the interview, I realized that customers are disloyal to brands for the same reasons. Twenty years as a counselor had convinced this person that men don't cheat because the other person is more attractive. Ninety-two percent of men said they cheated because they felt underappreciated in their current marriage. In other words, the other person made them feel special.

Apple and other customer service champs are successful because they make customers feel special. They approach with a warm welcome, they ask questions, they listen, they enhance the conversation, and they give you a feeling of empowerment. You leave the interaction with a smile on your face, with the confidence to conquer the world. Steve Jobs once said that life is too short to live someone else's dream. I would add that life is too short to hang around people—or brands—that pull you down instead of building you up. If you can make your customers feel appreciated, confident, and admired, they'll reward you with your loyalty. It's good for marriages. It's good for your brand, too.

CHECKOUT

1. **Study the five steps of service.** Review Apple's five steps of service and evaluate how you could incorporate each step in your business whether you run a physical location or a virtual service.

2. **Train your staff to follow the five steps.** If you manage staff, hold training sessions on the five steps of service. Develop mock scenarios where employees play the roles of the customer and the salesperson. Show them what the five steps really look and sound like. Send them the list, but don't forget to practice and model the behavior, too.

3. **Conduct your own research.** Start observing the difference for yourself. Walk into an Apple, LEGO, or AT&T retail store, and watch the interactions. See how those interactions compare to other stores that do not follow the model.

CHAPTER 9

Reset Your Customer's Internal Clock

Customers shouldn't think of your business as a place to buy a product or use a service. It should be a fun place to be!
—Richard Branson

Time slows down in a busy Apple Store. Employees work on a noncommissioned floor, which means there is no pressure to sell you a product quickly and to show you the door. By reducing the pressure customers feel when they're in the store, Apple has built the world's most profitable retail experience. It's astonishing that more businesses haven't caught on to this very simple principle! Some retail employees work for stores that do not have a commission structure but their bonuses are contingent upon meeting quotas. Managers at Apple Retail Stores know the monthly numbers they are supposed to reach, but the pressure to make those numbers rarely infiltrates the sales floor. The focus is on building relationships, and as a result, monthly sales goals are often met or exceeded. Apple has figured out what Isadore Sharp had discovered years earlier when he founded

Four Seasons Hotels: customers who feel happy and relaxed will reward your brand with their business and their loyalty.

In today's competitive global environment, people are stressed, hurried, and in many cases, forced to do more with fewer resources. Many customers are discouraged, tired, and grumpy. They certainly don't want to feel that way outside of work. Apple has an interesting challenge—how does a store with thousands of visitors a week turn discouraged, tired, and grumpy customers into inspired, energized, and happy ones? Store design is part of the solution, and we will address the topic in Part III. But an even more important element to creating an unhurried environment involves improving the communication between customers and staff in a way that alters customers' perceptions of time spent waiting for service.

Altering the Perception of Time

One major U.S. retailer that has emulated the Apple model—and has the customer service scores to prove it—shared an internal study with me that proves the value of resetting internal clocks. The research was so overwhelming that the store's managers coach employees to follow the method in each and every transaction, and the store has tens of thousands of employees in North America.

Here's what the retailer learned: when customers are greeted with a warm, friendly welcome, their perception of how long they wait is positively altered and their overall experience is enhanced significantly. Recall we already discussed the importance of a warm greeting in the Apple steps of service, but now it's important to expand on this and discuss how the greeting makes a difference in resetting clocks.

The internal research trial was conducted with two groups of customers. The first group was greeted by a friendly, smiling employee within seconds of walking through the door. They waited exactly three minutes for a salesperson to help them. The other group was not greeted and waited exactly the same amount of time. Both groups of customers were asked, "How promptly were you served?" The first group—the ones who had been greeted—said they spent less time waiting than those customers in the second group. Their perception of time had been altered. They had been given permission to slow down from their harried lives, take a deep breath, and enjoy the experience.

Altering the perception of time was just one benefit of greeting a customer. In the previous study, the customers were also asked, "On a scale from 1 to 10, how likely are you to recommend [retailer]?" By now you can probably guess which group gave the higher score.

One of the keys to resetting your customer's internal clock is to be specific. Don't be vague. It's not enough to say, "I'll be right with you." Instead say, "I'm finishing up with this customer, and I'll be with you in five minutes. If there's someone who can help you even sooner, I'll send them right over." If the customer had already been waiting five minutes, her internal clock has now been reset and is starting again.

Why You'll Never Wait More Than Three Minutes in an Apple Store

Apple also knows that approaching customers with a warm, friendly greeting is one of the easiest and most effective ways of slowing down a customer's internal clock. If done correctly, customers who have waited fifteen minutes for assistance will think they waited no more than a few minutes. Here is how a typical scenario might play out at an especially busy Apple Store where expectations about when service can be provided are set quickly and effectively.

> **Employee (Apple Specialist):** Hi, welcome to Apple. How can we help you today?
>
> **Customer:** I'm thinking of getting an iPad, and I'd like to take a look at them.
>
> **Employee:** Great. My name is Melinda. And your name?
>
> **Customer:** Carmine.
>
> **Employee:** Carmine, nice to meet you. As you can see, the store is really busy right now. Do me a favor and head over to the iPad table and just start playing with the devices. Have fun. If I can get to you next, I will.

But if you see someone free, grab them. I'll also let the other Specialists know that you would like their help, and one of them will get to you as soon as possible. But play with the iPad. There are videos, games, and a whole lot more already on the device. Will that be OK?

Customer: Sure. How long will it be? It's really crowded.

Employee: It is busy. It will be at least three to five minutes before I can get over here. I do have a manager on the floor right now, and I'll let him know that you are here. He will start seeing who else he can free up. But again, it will be at least three to five minutes. He will, however, touch base with you to make sure you're taken care of.

The manager in this scenario now owns the relationship. It's his job to make sure someone assists the customer as soon as possible. It's also his job to reset the customer's internal clock back to zero. The manager should check back with the customer (wherever the customer has wandered in the store) after approximately three to five minutes (the time expectation initially offered) to give that customer a status report or the help the customer came for.

So here is what happened in this scenario. The customer walked into a busy store and assumed he would wait an eternity, which, with few exceptions, would be the case at any other store. The experience at the Apple Store was different, however, because the customer felt appreciated as soon as he stepped inside. His internal clock had been reset, and the pace of his life slowed down. This is a critical psychological concept. A simple acknowledgment gives the customer the feeling that he is in the game. The customer knows he has been seen and is part of the "lineup." If the customer is not greeted and has to wait three minutes, the scene turns ugly very quickly. The customer becomes agitated. Pent-up frustrations from the day rise to the surface, and everybody loses. But just from having been greeted and acknowledged, the customer is willing to wait patiently for quite a while.

When Melinda, the Apple employee, told the customer that it would take three to five minutes before she could help him, she set the customer's clock to zero and his "timer" started again. The customer then started playing with the iPad, which was powered on, working, and loaded with applications. (Broken devices are fixed or replaced immediately in Apple Stores. How often do you find this attentiveness in other device stores? Not often.) Perhaps the customer discovered something on his own that he didn't know before about the iPad. His internal clock got reset again. When other Specialists or employees walked by the customer, some smiled and said hello. The customer doesn't realize it, but his internal clock got reset yet again. Finally, the manager walked over after several minutes to reset the clock one more time.

If you asked the customer in this scenario how long he had waited for a salesperson, what do you think his answer would be? Ten minutes? Wrong. He would say, "Two or three minutes." It's because he was greeted immediately, and the manager, the "owner" of the relationship returned to reset his internal clock. Once the manager tells the customer that he is next in line or he will have to wait three minutes for assistance, the customer perceives that he has waited only a few minutes to be served. He leaves the store thinking, *Great service. Fast and efficient!*

This concept of resetting internal clocks is such a critical component of the Apple experience, that it is discussed constantly at Apple stores. Managers are consistently watching and coaching employees to reset clocks.

> *If every retail store had customer service like Apple, the world would be a better place.* —Michael M.

How to Lose $70,000 in Five Minutes

Failing to reset clocks could cost you business. Most people hate the experience of buying a car because they feel pressured by commissioned salespeople. Instead of resetting clocks, their clocks get overwound! My close friend Tim and his wife, Denise, had the opposite experience at a car dealership, but equally as frustrating.

Tim and Denise ended up buying a new Mercedes because someone at another dealership, Audi, had not followed the Apple steps of service nor reset their internal clocks. Tim and Denise had no knowledge of the Apple steps of service; all they knew was that their experience at the dealership had been so horrible that they left, went to a competitor, and bought a car that day. But after listening to their story, it was obvious that failing to follow Apple's five steps, especially the greeting, cost Audi $70,000 in business. Here's what happened.

My friends had narrowed down their choices for a new car between two brands, Audi and Mercedes. Although they were impressed with the Mercedes, it was a higher price point than the Audi, and having owned an Audi in the past, they appreciated its quality. So they walked into an Audi dealership with a check in hand ready to buy a new car. The receptionist never looked up. They waited for a few minutes clearly in view of the receptionist. The receptionist didn't make eye contact, didn't smile, nor even acknowledge their presence. When Tim and Denise finally asked to a see a salesperson, the receptionist said that since they "didn't have an appointment," nobody was available at the time. They were told that if they waited, someone "might" be able to help them in forty-five minutes!

Tim and his wife were confused because they had never heard of such a policy at an auto dealer. Perhaps, if the receptionist had offered an explanation, they would have understood. But no explanation was given. They decided to leave, and the receptionist didn't even say good-bye. Tim and Denise then went directly to the Mercedes dealership down the street where a salesperson, Alan, greeted them with a warm welcome right away. No more than five minutes had elapsed from the moment they walked into the door before they were "sold." They were so satisfied with the experience that they bought a Mercedes that day, spent more than they would have spent at Audi, and even recommended Alan by name to other friends in the market for a car.

Audi lost a sale because its employee was not trained in the Apple way. Here's how the conversation would have gone at the Audi dealership with an effectively trained receptionist.

Receptionist (within a few feet or seconds of the couple walking through the door)**:** Hi, welcome to Audi. How can we help you today?

Customer: We're here to look at a new car.

Receptionist: Great. We'd love to help you. We have started a new "by appointment" program at our store so you can make an appointment to come in at a specific time. However, since you're here, let me try to find someone who can help you right away.

Customer: Thanks. (starts looking around)

Receptionist (two minutes later)**:** Our sales reps are really busy today with customers. "Fred" can see you just as soon as he's done with his current customer. We want to be respectful of your time, so I have to tell you that he will not be available for forty-five minutes. If you can wait, Fred will help you. But I'll keep looking, and if someone is available even sooner, I'll send them over right away. Can I offer you some coffee or something to drink in the meantime?

Customer: I guess that's fine. We didn't want to wait that long, but since we're here we might as well stay. (The customer is still disappointed and grudgingly accepts the wait time, but at least he has been acknowledged and his clock has been set. He's in the game.)

Receptionist (five minutes later)**:** Has anyone helped you yet?

Customer: No, we're still waiting.

Receptionist: Let me check on Fred's status. I'll be right back.

Receptionist (three minutes later)**:** Fred is still with another customer, but Marvin is almost free. He will be with you in less than fifteen minutes. While you wait for Marvin, would you like to see our new sedan? It's been named car of the year. It's an amazing experience. Feel free to sit inside and check it out.

Marvin (ten minutes later)**:** Hi, I'm Marvin. Please accept my apologies for the wait.

Customer: No problem. We were waiting for only a few minutes.

The customers had not been waiting "a few minutes." The couple had been waiting close to thirty minutes, but their internal clocks had been reset several times. I ran this "Apple" version of the scenario by my friends, Tim and Denise, and they agreed that if such a conversation had taken place, they would have stayed and purchased the car they originally intended to buy. The car dealership could have made $70,000 in one transaction simply by resetting a customer's internal clock. Instead, the dealership lost the sale, and my friends became vocal detractors of the brand to friends and family. Now, if you think about it even more carefully, this sale was lost well before the receptionist failed to follow the Apple steps of service. It was lost in the hiring process, which is why Chapter 2 is critical. The receptionist never smiled. She was unfriendly. In other words, Apple never would have hired her! You can train people to greet, smile, and reset internal clocks, but if they are naturally unfriendly, the five steps mean nothing.

Minimizing Frustration at the Happiest Place on Earth

Resetting the clock is not a new concept in other areas of customer service. Apple simply applies it to the communication between the customer and salesperson. But many companies reset the clock, especially in the areas of phone and tech support. Amazon, Symantec, AT&T, and many other brands will let you know what the wait time is when you call for help. AT&T and Amazon phone reps ask customers for permission before putting them on hold and will get back on the phone every minute or two to offer a status update. Visit the support page for Symantec, which makes the popular Norton antivirus suite of products, and the wait time is clearly posted on the website for its 24-7 phone support (Amazon offers this as well). Think about it. What would leave you feeling better about the conversation, sitting on hold for six minutes or being told up front that the wait time will be six minutes? The latter, of course.

Disney has more experience than any brand in creating smiles. But as many of the 30 million visitors a year to Walt Disney World can tell you, the "happiest place on earth" experience can be compromised by standing in long, long lines. The smartphone era has bred a generation of impatient guests, and Disney is constantly working on its customer service to stay relevant and to improve the overall experience.

Disney technicians and Imagineers (the folks who come up with ideas for new rides and attractions) have had to develop ways to keep people informed and entertained during their wait. Although Disney doesn't use the phrase "reset internal clocks," it's exactly what they do when they dispatch Captain Jack Sparrow to entertain people when a line gets too long. Yes, there is actually a nerve center under Cinderella's Castle with flat screen TVs showing wait times at all the attractions. Technicians will even launch miniparades to keep guests occupied or to siphon people to a less-congested part of the park. If a restaurant is too busy, technicians will dispatch "greeters" to hand out menus to people in line. They are even experimenting with offering short video games (about 90 seconds in length) to keep people occupied while they are waiting. The goal at Disney, of course, is to make its guests happy, and Disney has found that the less time you *perceive* waiting in line, the happier you'll be.

Three Simple Secrets of Customer Service Champs

If you study the great customer service brands of our time, including The Ritz Carlton, Four Seasons Hotels, Zappos, Nordstrom, Starbucks, FedEx, and Apple, you will find a common theme. Each brand has learned that customers or guests want three things— smart staff, a friendly face, and fast service.

- **Smart.** Smart means that the staff is knowledgeable. Everyone on the Apple floor knows about the products. Some are more specialized than others and focus on certain areas or product categories, but they can all explain the products. In Part III you'll learn about a soap company called Lush that sends a sample of all new products to every employee so each one can speak about each new product from personal experience.

- **Friendly.** Friendly people greet you with a smile, offer their name, ask for yours in return, use your name during the conversation, give their undivided attention, have a positive attitude, and walk you to the door as though you were a guest in their home.

- **Fast.** Fast service should not be interpreted as getting a customer in and out as fast as possible. Fast is as fast as the customer wants the experience to be! If an Apple customer walks into a store and says, "I'm on my lunch break, and I don't have that much time," an Apple employee will serve that person as promptly as possible. But if another customer wants to spend a leisurely amount of time to learn about a MacBook and it takes an hour to answer all his questions, that's OK as well. Remember, Apple Store employees are told constantly that their goal is not to sell stuff. The goal is to make people's lives better. It is to enrich a customer's life and have her walk out with a smile. For some folks, a smile means in and out in five minutes. For others, a smile takes an hour.

> I talked to Apple customer service for almost two hours. At least one and a half of that we discussed college football and not Apple products. —Ryan M.

Play Offense, Not Defense

My daughters love to bring their prized possessions in the car whenever we travel. The problem: they often drop things in the cracks of their seats and then scream at the driver (usually me or my wife) because they can't reach the Polly Pocket shoe, the skirt to their Zhu Zhu Pet, or whatever else they decided to lug in the car that day. It's not our fault when they lose their trinkets, but we get the anger, blame, and frustration.

These childish behaviors (defensiveness, blame, dismissive expressions or gestures, and little effort to remedy the mishap) are expected in a four-year-old, but unfortunately, they have become all too common in the way employees often deal with customers who have legitimate questions about the service. Have you ever heard one of these comments in response to a customer service question?

- "That's our policy, and I can't do anything about it."

- "I don't work in that department and can't help you with that."

- "I just got back from break and know nothing about this."

- "He's new and doesn't know what he's doing yet."

- "You can't use that coupon because it expired yesterday."

- "No one has ever had an issue with this before."

- "I'm helping someone else right now."

Customer service blunders are inevitable. Customers complain, and there will be times they have to wait, no matter where they are. Resetting your customer's clock is even more important in these delicate situations. Salespeople need to be smart, friendly, and fast. They also need to be skilled at smoothing things over for disgruntled customers. The process works much better if employees are trained to go on the offense instead of playing defense.

My wife writes a customer service column on our site, and she receives great customer service stories from people around the country. Here's one story of how an Outback Steakhouse in Louisville, Colorado, played offense and hit a home run.

My wife and I entered an Outback Steakhouse one evening for a quick dinner. The hostess took our name and the need for a table for two. As we sat there, additional parties came in and then we noticed a trend. Numerous parties of three and four were being seated but we were not—the bypassing of us for larger parties continued past the time when we should have been given a larger table. Once I addressed the issue with the manager on duty, we were quickly seated, with a sincere apology and an appetizer "on the house." At that point, we were satisfied with the quick response and enjoyed our free appetizer.

As it turns out, the owner of this and several other Outback locations was in the building and came over to our table, offered a sincere apology, and indicated that the hostess was new and that he had replaced her for the evening and would provide her with additional training. He took the blame, placing it on himself as a training failure instead of the typical "blame it on the employee" response. He then asked if he could talk to us again after our meal and offered to buy our desserts.

He spent twenty minutes talking to us, gathering our opinion on a number of topics related to his restaurant and our overall observations and experience. This was a great way to handle such a simple service failure, well beyond what we expected. We were happy after the free appetizer and even more so after the free desserts and the personal attention from the owner.

But the purpose of this tale is what happened next—the owner picked up the tab for our entire meal, asking only that we tip the waitperson on the total bill. This was a fantastic response for having us wait a bit longer than we should have for a table and a great example of dealing with a customer service failure. Then he totally blew us away…he handed us a card and offered to buy us another complete meal, an appetizer, two entrées, two drinks, and two desserts, if we would come back two weeks from that night, give them another try, and give our comments to the duty manager that evening.[1]

Vanessa usually paraphrases stories she mentions in her articles, but she couldn't trim this one, nor could I. This Outback owner could start a customer service training school for restaurant managers and waitstaff! Now I challenge all customer service professionals to stay off the defense for a change and go to this measure every time a customer is unhappy. If you do, you are sure to reset your customers' clocks, strengthen their perceptions of your brand, and keep them for life.

If your staff is not greeting customers and resetting internal clocks, then shut this book now and schedule a training session to coach your team right away on this very important skill. Go ahead. I can wait. Nothing else in the book will matter if your staff doesn't understand or cannot execute the steps in Chapters 8 and 9. Part III will be a waste of time, like putting lipstick on a pig. But take your time. When you come back, we'll pick up where we left off and, in Chapter 10, discuss the content of the sales conversation.

1. **Review all of your customer touchpoints.** Are you and your staff greeting customers warmly? Are you making them feel as though they have entered an organized, helpful environment? Are you letting them know how long it will take to address their needs or answer questions?

2. **Train your staff to reset internal clocks.** If you manage a business of any type with a physical location or phone support, every person on your team must be coached in the five steps and in the proper way to reset their customers' perception of time.

3. **Provide training consistently.** Apple managers are providing constant feedback or praise for their staff. AT&T managers hold coaching sessions once a week where they review the greeting and even conduct role-playing exercises to make sure every employee is proficient at providing a superior customer experience.

CHAPTER 10

Sell the Benefit

People don't just want to buy personal computers anymore. They want to know what they can do with them, and we're going to show people exactly that.

—Steve Jobs

My mother-in-law, Patty Cook, expressed an interest in buying an iPad for her husband, Ken. As we approached the holiday season, she contacted me for advice. Sensing a unique opportunity to do some observational research, I told her that we should visit the Apple Store and ask a Specialist for advice. I purposely avoided offering any input, and I did not say a word when we walked into the store. It was important for me to watch the interaction and how it impacted Patty, without influencing her decision in any way. Patty is friendly and talkative, so it should not have been difficult for an Apple employee to walk Patty through the steps of service. She also knows very little about Apple products or computers in general, so she needed basic information. We had two conversations with two separate Apple employees. The results were very, very different.

The first thing I learned was that Apple gets it right more often than it gets it wrong, but it gets it wrong from time to time. Everything in this book is aspirational. The concepts you're reading will help you create an exceptional experience for your customers whether you sell a product or a service in-store, on the web, or over the phone. It's my contention that Apple has refined the customer service model to the highest degree of any major corporation, but with 30,000 employees around the world, even Apple has a difficult time achieving its ideal experience in each and every transaction, especially if someone on the sales floor does not get trained repeatedly in the five steps. Here are two examples—one where it went wrong and another when it went right.

When It Went Wrong

In the first store we met a Specialist, Alba, who did not walk through the steps of service, and she did not score any points with Patty. See if you can figure out why.

> **Patty:** Hi, I'm thinking of buying an iPad for my husband. Can you tell me more about it?[1]
>
> **Alba:** Well, there are two models. One connects you to Wi-Fi and the other to 3G, so you can get an Internet connection anywhere. Those start at $629.

Patty is thoroughly confused less than one minute into the conversation. She's acknowledged she is nontechnical. Patty doesn't know what Wi-Fi or 3G means. She doesn't even know what to ask next, and Alba is not guiding her.

> **Patty:** Is this your top of the line? (Does Patty really need "top of the line"? Alba never probed to find out.)
>
> **Alba:** This is the iPad 2. All the different models we carry do exactly the same thing.

It's only the storage space that's different. It goes 16 gigs, 32 gigs, and 64 gigs.

By now, Patty has the "deer-in-the-headlights" look: totally befuddled. I feel horrible because I told Patty that buying an Apple product would be a memorable experience. I'm debating whether or not to jump in and end the misery. I let it go to see what would happen next. Yes, I know, bad son-in-law!

Patty: My husband is a photographer, and he wants to store his prints on it.

Alba: He can definitely do that. (Long pause. Nobody speaks. It's getting painful to watch.)

Patty: Would you recommend one over the other?

Alba: Like I said, they all do the same thing. The only difference is storage space, and if you want one with Wi-Fi or 3G.

At this point, my six-year-old daughter, who was also with us, saved all of us by loudly proclaiming, "I have to go potty!" She wasn't the only one who needed relief. Patty and I left the store without having made a purchase or being "enriched." Patty was thoroughly confused, and Apple had failed to make a sale or establish a relationship with a new customer. Where did Alba go wrong? Here are a few factors:

- Alba explained the features of the product, but not the benefits. Nobody cares about features. They care about how the product or service will improve their lives.

- Alba failed to probe. She didn't ask questions to guide the conversation. When Patty asked if the iPad was "top of the line," a well-trained Apple Specialist would be concerned about whether the product was the right one for her and not try to sell her the most expensive model. Remember, Steve Jobs once said that he doesn't give customers what they want. He gives them what they need.

- Alba never made an effort to connect with any of us emotionally. She never asked for Patty's name, my name, or anything about Patty's six-year-old granddaughter who was sitting right next to us laughing and giggling as she was playing on an iPad. She could have at least said, "Your granddaughter can play on your husband's iPad when she comes to visit!"

I convinced Patty to do some other shopping, get her head together, and return later to the Apple Store with the hope that we could score a Specialist who had had better training. This time we were greeted by Jessica, who had been trained in the five steps of service. The experience for Patty was wildly different and far more satisfying.

When It Went Right

Patty: I want to get an iPad for my husband. Can you just tell me a little about them?

Jessica: Absolutely. Sure. No problem. The great functionality of the iPad is how portable the device is. You can surf the web, play games, check e-mails, take pictures, store movies—there's a whole lot you can do.

Patty: He loves to search the Internet and to play games. But I want to get him on the couch next to me instead of going in the other room to play his online poker.

Jessica: Exactly (laughing). This will do the trick! Do you have a wireless Internet connection?

Patty: No, but my son has mentioned we would need to get one. He can set it up.

Jessica: The reason I ask is because there are two different types of iPads. There's one just with Wi-Fi to connect to a wireless Internet connection, whether it be through your home network or free at a Starbucks or any place with Wi-Fi. But there's also the iPad with Wi-Fi plus 3G. What the 3G capability allows you to do is connect to the Internet anywhere.

Patty: He might like that. He's a photographer who wants to go to conventions and show his photos.

Jessica: If he's traveling, 3G is great because he'll be connected to the Internet via cell signal. From there you have to think about the storage capacity, the amount of space you have on the device, the amount of things you can store. Pictures take up a lot of storage. Music, movies, all take up storage. Our base model is 16 gigabytes of capacity. That will store an average of a few thousand songs. A full-length HD movie takes up about 2 to 3 gigs so it's already taking up storage.

Patty: I don't think he'll watch movies. It's more about the photos.

Jessica: Gotcha. Then you'll want to consider either the 16 GB or the 32 GB model. The 32 GB might be best because it offers the extra storage. There is no way to increase the amount of storage built into the device. I recommend shooting high so he has the extra room for his photographs.

Patty: So what was the one that's always connected?

Jessica: Wi-Fi plus 3G. The data plans are offered either through AT&T or Verizon.

I could tell Patty was already sold on the 32 GB model. But Jessica wasn't done. She was about to close the sale with a wow moment, adding a nugget of information that would impress Patty and directly relate to something that Patty had mentioned earlier in the conversation. "Come with me," said Jessica as she led Patty to the accessory wall at the back of the store. "This is a camera connection kit. Your husband can take his photographs, remove the memory card, insert it in this slot, and transfer his photos to the iPad." Patty was thrilled. I could tell the sale had been made. But Jessica had one more thing...

"There's one more thing for you to consider," she said. Once he opens his new iPad, you can tell your husband that we offer free classes right in the store if he'd like to learn how to use it." Steve Jobs, who was famous for surprising his audiences with "one more thing" at the end of his presentations, would have been proud.

Patty and I left the store because we had another appointment, but the sale had been made. Patty bought an iPad 2 a few days later (the 32 GB model that Jessica had recommended). Ken was a very happy customer on the morning of December 25. Patty felt bad because Jessica didn't get the sale. I told Patty that Apple Store employees are not on commission, and Jessica would not be penalized for the time she spent with Patty. She did her job, she did it well, and Patty was happy. That's all that matters to Jessica. What did Jessica do right?

- Jessica talked about benefits, not features. Instead of using terms like 3G and Wi-Fi, Jessica went directly to what Patty (and Ken) could do with the device: enjoy games, e-mail, photos, movies, and so on. It was in that moment that Patty smiled and began warming up to the idea of purchasing an iPad. She wasn't confused. She was empowered. She began to enjoy the sales process. Jessica had created a relationship. Once you build a relationship, your customer will make it easier for you to make a sale.

- Jessica probed with simple questions to understand Patty's situation and how Ken would use the device.

- Jessica listened closely and used what she had heard to create a wow moment, introducing Patty to the camera connection kit.

Here's the kicker. Remember, I said that Patty likes to talk and strike up conversations. Patty was so satisfied with this experience that she actually asked Jessica if she could pass along a recommendation to her manager. I was surprised—but I guess I shouldn't have been—when Jessica said, "Thanks. But as long as you're happy that's all that matters." Patty persisted, but Jessica stuck to her ground—thanks, but no thanks.

The fact that Jessica declined an opportunity for a customer to praise her in front of her boss should strike fear in the hearts of business owners everywhere. It tells you everything you need to know about why the Apple Stores are succeeding and why you might be falling behind when it comes to customer service. Ask yourself honestly if a customer tells one of your employees that she thought so highly of the customer experience that she would like to speak to a manager, would your employees bust down the door to the manager's office to show off a satisfied customer? Sure, they would. The reason Jessica did not want Patty to talk to the manager is because it would teach the manager nothing new. It's *expected* that store employees create magical moments on the sales floor all day long. Jessica's manager wouldn't get any work done if she dragged every happy customer into his office! I've asked Apple Store employees why Jessica didn't jump at the opportunity. They all said because it happens to each of them every day. It's all part of the Apple show. Would the person who plays the character of Cinderella at Disneyland rush to her supervisor to say, "Did you see the smile I put on that little girl's face! I must be really good." Of course not. Magical moments are expected all the time at Disney and the Apple Store.

"Was your life enriched by our Apple experience?" I asked Patty.

"Yes, it was," Patty confirmed.

"When you fill out the e-mail survey that Apple will send, will you say that you would recommend Apple to someone else?"

"Yes, definitely," Patty responded.

That's what matters to Apple.

What Your Customers Really Love

Apple employees talk benefits, not features. Apple dedicated itself to communicating benefits with the opening of its first store in 2001. At the time retailers were finding opportunities to talk to their customers less; Apple decided to talk to their customers more. "We found ways to strike up a conversation at every possible opportunity. We talk while they play with products on the tables. And when they join us for a workshop. These conversations have taught us that customers love our products, but what they really want is to make a scrapbook out of family photos. They want to make a movie about their kid. Or a website about traveling across the country."[2]

Steve Jobs wasn't passionate about computers. He was passionate about building elegantly designed and simple-to-use tools that would help people unleash their personal creativity. The most effective Apple employees—and the best salespeople in any company for that matter—focus on the needs of the customers and how the product or service will improve their lives.

When I walked into the Apple Store near the Paris Opera—one of the most beautiful Apple Stores in the world—I asked a specialist named Philippe about the new iPhone 4S that had recently been introduced.

"Philippe, why should I get one of these new phones instead of sticking with the iPhone 4, which suits me just fine?" I asked.

"The iPhone 4S is our best phone yet," he said. "It's faster, has better graphics, and takes better photographs and video." Not once did he mention the specs of the A5 chip, which makes it all possible, because Philippe knew that speeds and feeds don't matter to most consumers as much as what those specs mean to their daily lives. I found it remarkable that 6,000 miles from Apple headquarters in Cupertino, California, a Specialist in France could communicate as clearly and effectively as sales floor Specialists in Apple's Silicon Valley stores. Sell the benefit—every Apple employee gets the message.

Few people care that the iPhone 4S has a dual-core A5 chip. Technically speaking, the A5 chip "contains a rendition of a chip based upon the dual-core ARM Cortex-A9 MPCore CPU with NEON SIMD accelerator and a dual core PowerVR SGX543MP2 GPU."[3] Does the previous explanation inspire you to run out and buy a new phone today? Of course not. It's not inspiring, because it's not about you. It's about the technology. Customers would never see such an explanation in Apple's marketing material nor would they hear anything nearly as technical spoken by Apple Store employees. Instead, they might hear something similar to Philippe's conversation: Our new A5 chip makes everything faster—browsing the web, going from app to app, gaming, and doing just about everything.

When Apple sent an e-mail to millions of customers introducing its new iPhone 4S, the first sentence of the e-mail said that the iPhone 4S was Apple's most amazing iPhone yet. Why? Because of Siri, among the other features. Technically speaking, Siri is an intelligent software assistant and knowledge navigator application in iOS 5 that uses a natural language user interface to answer questions. The previous sentence is accurate, but far too technical to inspire must customers. It doesn't answer the question, "Why should I care?" Instead, Apple marketing material described Siri as, "The intelligent assistant you can ask to make calls, send texts, set reminders, and more." Now that's easy to understand, memorable, and compelling. It sells the benefit.

Why Should I Care?

When I studied journalism at Northwestern's Medill School of Journalism, the first concept we were taught in Journalism 101 was to answer the question, "Why should your readers care?" The same technique applies to the conversation you have about your company, product, service, or cause. Nobody cares about the product as much as they care about what the product will do for them.

Apple Store employees are trained to sell the benefit behind Apple's products, just as Steve Jobs did so brilliantly in his presentations. Jobs always answered the question, "Why should you care?" I now encourage my clients to have a clear and concise answer to that question and to train their sales staff to have the same answer as well. I recall working with the CEO of a medical device manufacturer to create the message behind his company's revolutionary new CT scan machine.

"Can you tell me about the new machine?" I asked.

"It's the world's first dynamic volume CT scan that utilizes 320 ultra-high resolution rows to image an entire organ in a single gantry rotation," the CEO said proudly.

"Let me rephrase the question," I said. "So what?"

"Well, it means if you suffer a stroke, doctors can use our machine to make a much faster, more accurate diagnosis, which could mean the difference between going home and living a full life or never recognizing your family again."

"Now I'm interested! Why didn't you say that before?" I asked.

"I guess I never thought about it that way," he said.

Start thinking about it that way. Nobody cares about your product or service. They care about what your product or service will do for them. Selling the benefit plays a big role in the Apple experience. Make sure it plays a prominent role in your experience as well.

CHECKOUT

1. **Always ask the question, "Why should I care?"** Communicate the benefits behind your product by answering the following question: Why should my customers care? Remember, it's not about you: it's about them.

2. **Communicate consistently.** Include the answer to the question you just answered in all of your marketing collateral, websites, advertisements, and presentations.

3. **Train everyone to sell the benefit.** Finally, make sure each and every employee is trained to focus on the customers' needs and to clearly articulate the benefits behind each of your core products or services.

Unleash Your Customer's Inner Genius

I think people who buy Macs are the creative spirits in this world. They are out to change the world, and we make tools for those kinds of people.
—Steve Jobs

I f you talk to Apple employees long enough they begin to sound a lot like Robert Redford in *The Horse Whisperer*. Redford's character, Tom Booker, speaks in short pearls of wisdom. Here are some quotes from the movie followed by actual remarks I've heard from Apple employees.

Tom Booker: I don't help people with horse problems. I help horses with people problems.

Apple Genius: We don't fix computers. We repair relationships.

Tom Booker: When I work with a horse, it's no good just me doing it. The owner's got to be involved, too.

Apple Specialist: It's not good enough for me to solve the problem. I want to empower you to find a solution.

Tom Booker: When I work with a horse, I want to know its history. I try to figure out what's going on in its head.

Apple Manager: We don't hire people because they were great trainers at another company. We hire people who can get inside the head of a customer.

Tom Booker: It's not a question if you can. You are.

Apple Creative: Don't say you can't. You can.

In the movie, Tom Booker helps a traumatized teenager find the confidence to ride her horse again after a tragic accident. On the Apple Store stage, Specialists, Creatives, and Geniuses play the role of Tom Booker by helping people discover their inner strengths and providing them the tools and the education to reach their potential.

One Apple Specialist told me that a customer, an older man, once kissed him on the cheek before he left the store. The customer

Apple employee teaching a customer something new. *Source: Getty Images*

was anxious about using computers. His kids, who seemed to be the know-it-all types, were frustrated with their dad's lack of knowledge and would roll their eyes when he asked questions. When the kids went to another part of the store, the Specialist showed the father something on the Mac that even his kids didn't know. When the kids returned a few minutes later, the father proudly showed them what he had learned. Their jaws dropped, the dad had a big grin on his face, and he ended the transaction by planting a kiss on the employee's cheek. In this case the *customer* gave the employee a "fond farewell" he would always remember!

Building Relationships One to One

One to One is a membership program at the Apple Retail Store designed to help you get the most out of Apple's products. For $99, upon the purchase of a new Mac, Apple customers can sign up for one year of personalized classes. The classes are made by appointment and conducted face-to-face in an Apple Store with Creatives who are trained to give instruction on Apple products and software. Customers can learn just about anything: basics about the Mac operating system; how to design a website; enjoying, sharing, and editing photos or movies; creating a presentation; and much more. One to One offers several ways to learn: one-hour personal visits with a trainer, small group workshops, or longer blocks of time where multiple customers work on their own personal projects while a trainer checks in to see how they're doing.

The One to One program was created to help build customers for life. It was designed on the premise that the more you understand a product, the more you enjoy it, and the more likely you are to build a long-term relationship with the company. And don't forget that the more you like a product and the relationship you've experienced with the company, the more likely you are to recommend the product or service to someone else.

Instructors are trained to provide guidance and instruction, but also to inspire customers, giving them the tools to make them more creative than they ever imagined. Apple doesn't sell One to One as an unnecessary add-on to boost its bottom line. One to One is a critical component of the Apple experience, which is why it is always offered and discussed with customers as a benefit to purchasing a Mac. In my own experience, the Apple Keynote presentation software has opened up a new way for me to think about the presentations I give and how I instruct clients on telling stories through presentations. When I first learned Keynote, I tried to read a manual, but it wasn't nearly as empowering as when I sat side-by-side with a Creative who helped me unleash my "inner presentation genius."

You might recall meeting Carolyn DiPiero in Part I. She is the retired schoolteacher from Modesto, California, who bought her first Mac primarily because of the interactions she experienced in the store. DiPiero signed up for the One to One training program and took full advantage of it, scheduling sessions to learn everything she could about the platform and its software. When I asked DiPiero what she remembers from the sessions, she recalled how Creatives built her confidence through personal conversations. They made her feel that they, too, were in her place at one time and if they could learn, so could she. Many of them actually were in her shoes. I've met several Apple Store employees who were inspired to apply for the company after they took One to One classes. Some became Creatives, others aspired to be Creatives, and others became Specialists on the sales floor or on the management track. How many companies do you know that make such a profound influence on their customers that many of those customers end up working for the company? If you can inspire people to feel better about themselves and their abilities—and to discover abilities they didn't even know they had—those people are going to be loyal to you and evangelize your brand.

The trainers must have made an impression on DiPiero, because she vividly remembers details of their personal lives:

> I learned that Stewart, who was in his forties, used to be a teacher. Jimmy was a little younger, under thirty. Jimmy had an interesting background. He used to teach classes for people who wanted to enter the ministry. Kirsten was a special-ed student in high school. She had a learning problem but overcame it with help from supportive parents. Now she teaches at Apple. Amazing story. And Eric was a motivator. I once said, "I feel stupid," and

Eric shot back, "Don't ever say that!" They are all so humble. They act like servants when they are really kings.[1]

Hiring plays a role in DiPiero's experience. Did you note that many of DiPiero's instructors were former teachers? Again, Apple does not hire for technical knowledge. It hires people for their attitude, personality, and ability to create memorable experiences. One former Apple Retail executive told me that early in the Apple Store history, Apple learned that former teachers made exceptional instructors as well as salespeople. Think about it this way—if parents ask a nineteen-year-old what is the best computer game for their child, he might lead those parents to the games he likes or the games that get the highest rating. A former third-grade teacher will ask, "Who is the game for? What are her interests?" A teacher is more likely to probe, ask the right questions, and ultimately give the customer a better recommendation. You'll see former teachers at Apple. But Apple also hires people as diverse as their customer base—young and old, quirky and straitlaced, every personality is represented. Apple celebrates diversity. Also remember the culture is created by design, not by default. Creatives understand that everyone has an inner genius that is desperate to reveal itself. Their job is to help you discover it.

One tactic Creatives use to help you find your inner genius is to encourage you to touch the computer. They point to items on the computer (always with two fingers, which is less threatening) and ask the customer to actually do the task. They will not grab the computer from the customer and do something themselves unless they ask permission first with phrases such as "May I touch the computer?" Creatives are trained to let the customer control the experience because it builds the customers' confidence and makes them more comfortable with the notion that they can accomplish a task they didn't know how to do when they walked into the session. The experience is fun, enjoyable, and empowering—an effective combination to win customers for life.

> *I used to think Disneyland should run the world. Now I think it's Apple!* —Carolyn D.

The Apple of Food Stores

For an Italian like myself, New York City's Eataly is food heaven. Thousands of customers have discovered this haven to every Italian food imaginable. There are fourteen Eataly partnerships around the world, including seven in Japan. The location in New York City, partly owned by celebrity chef Mario Batali, is enormous. It has seven restaurants with capacity for 300 diners. If you're looking for any kind of Italian food, Eataly has it: pastas, wines, olive oils, sauces, salamis, pastries, espressos, and cheese. It also offers cooking classes in its school, La Scuola.

On a trip to New York, I sat down with Eataly partner Nicola Farinetti and asked him to describe the vision behind his family's food empire. If you didn't know Farinetti was running an Italian food store, you'd think he was working for Apple. He talked about the importance of messaging and signage. He proudly described the importance of offering an uncluttered experience, despite hundreds of visitors a day. He talked openly about spending $250,000 a year on training employees in customer service skills. And Farinetti revealed why classes were so important. According to Farinetti, the more people know about the products, the more they enjoy their experience with the products and the brand. Sound familiar?

Instruction enhances the customer experience—for tech companies, food companies, or companies in nearly every category. The more Eataly's customers know about Italian food and understand the difference between olive oil from northern Italy and olive oil from the south, the more they will appreciate the product. When customers learn they really can make their own risotto, they feel empowered, confident, and proud. It creates a positive feeling that enhances the overall experience.

At Eataly, like Apple, the signage is also carefully considered. The signs are simple black letters on a white background, much like Apple signs. There are signs at every product station designed to teach customers something they didn't know. The signs describe everything from where the best Italian honeys are sourced (southern Italy) to where the art of Italian coffee roasting began (Piedmont). Farinetti's family has learned that customers are looking for more than food products; they are seeking an experience. The more they know, the more likely they are to enjoy the product.

I didn't enjoy wine until I learned to appreciate it through an enhanced experience. A friend in the wine business arranged an exclusive lunch with California wine pioneer Robert Mondavi. Listening to Mondavi regale us with stories about the history of California wine making and the nuances between varietals created a memorable experience for me. It also didn't hurt that we were tasting Mondavi's best wines on a sunny terrace overlooking the vineyard. All my senses were stimulated, adding to the experience. I learned that I could appreciate the difference between a California Cabernet and a French Bordeaux. The more confident I grew in my ability to understand the product, the more I enjoyed the product, and the more product I consumed!

The Apple Store Dance

Apple customers are free to express themselves in an Apple Store, and they have found a way to do so and share their quirkiness with thousands of other people. Search YouTube for the phrase "Apple Store dance," and you will find thousands of links of people who recorded themselves dancing in an Apple Store and then uploaded the video to the Internet. Apple has created an environment where people feel so welcome and comfortable that they'll do corny dances while employees and customers look on. They are accepted for who they are.

Some of the dances are very funny. One guy, dressed like Jennifer Lopez, sings her pop hit "On the Floor" while customers look on in the background. Lady Gaga's "Edge of Glory" seems to be another popular hit to dance to as well as Beyoncé's "Single Ladies." Justine Ezarik has the most popular clips. She's a young lady who has been dancing at the Apple Store for several years. One of her dance videos has more than 1.5 million views on YouTube! In the video she dances for about four minutes. It's especially humorous because an Apple employee helping a customer in the background glances at her once and then returns to talking to the customer about the iMac.[2]

The funniest thing about these videos is really not the song and dance but the customers and employees in the background. In most cases the employees smile and walk right by to help other customers just as they did with Justine. Since Apple employees are hired for personality themselves, they understand the desire that people have to express themselves. Obviously if someone is terribly disruptive, the person will be asked to stop the behavior or to leave the store, but more often than not Apple customers get away with it. Apple's goal is to be the leader in customer service worldwide, and if that means the stores act as vehicles through which customers express themselves and their individuality, so be it.

Apple Store Employees Talk About the Experience

In the United Kingdom, Apple Store employees created a video to discuss what it means to them personally to work for the brand. Their responses are very instructive and reinforce some of the core concepts in this chapter and this book.

- "The most important thing we do is making sure each customer that comes in gets the best experience possible"—Mark, Expert

- "The Apple Retail Experience is about the desire to connect with people. It's not to just sell a product but to invest in relationships."—Eliza-Jane, Specialist

- "When you sign on you are getting to be a part of something larger. We are part of the pioneers who actually make a difference in people's lives."—John, Business Manager

- "I know I make a difference working at Apple. I get to make a difference in people's lives. I get to enrich lives and to teach people. It's a really good feeling."—Logan, Specialist

- "Not only do I care about customers in and outside of the store. They also care about us. I don't see that anywhere else."—John, Specialist[3]

Yes, they do sound like Tom Booker. But that's the point. Apple Store employees are profoundly moved by their role, and they are especially touched when they inspire and elevate the customers' spirits.

The LEGO Experience

Recall from Chapter 8 the trip to the local mall where my daughters and I visited the LEGO Store right next to the Apple Store. We were greeted upon entering by a friendly employee, "John," who was greeting each and every visitor. When I asked John why he was doing it, he said, "That's my job—to greet everyone with a warm welcome." *Someone has been taking lessons from the Apple Store*, I thought to myself. The world's children spend 5 billion hours a year playing with LEGO construction bricks. My daughters, who had never played with LEGOs before this visit, spent one of those hours having the time of their lives in the store. The large glass windows and interactive models inside the store (as well as the greeter) attracted us into the store, but it was the experience that kept my kids there.

The LEGO Store is designed to encourage play and to facilitate the spontaneous joy of creation. Upon entering—and being greeted by John—my kids rushed to what LEGO calls "the living room," an interactive play area positioned in the center of the store designed for hands-on play. Their behavior was exactly what they had done a few minutes earlier when they walked into the Apple Store next door and began playing games on the iPads that were positioned in the center of the store.

While my daughters were proudly showing off their creations, I had a chance to speak with one of the employees, and I asked about the philosophy behind the interactive displays. "We're all about providing an awesome experience in the store because, (1) we want you to come back, and (2) we want you tell your family and friends about us." It didn't surprise me that LEGO employees were, like Apple, seeking a positive answer to the ultimate question—how likely are you to recommend the product to others? When I told the employee that the LEGO Store felt like the Apple Store, he said, "It's no coincidence that our locations are placed near or next to Apple Stores. We're trying to provide a similar experience."

Once the LEGO employee told me they were trying to provide an Apple-like experience, I began looking for other similarities. Sure enough, there was one: workshops. The Apple Store offers classes and workshops for groups of people who want to work on a project such as creating photo books, editing movies, and so on. Prior to leaving the LEGO Store, an employee told us about the free weekly building workshops held every Tuesday at 5:00 p.m. The workshops are called building events and have themes tied to the month in which the workshop is being held (e.g., rose for Mother's Day in May workshops, Santa for Christmas in December workshops). The kids learn to build the piece, and they get to take it home. Since we first visited the LEGO Store in November, my daughters wanted to return the following week to build a turkey model and they wanted Dad to take them. The LEGO experience had won them over.

If you really want to get your kids started early in the art of customer service, get them a LEGO Apple Store kit. Actually, the store model is good for kids and adults. Think about it. LEGO building is considered a great tool to jump-start creativity. The next time you hold a creative brainstorm on improving customer service, you might want to have the Apple Store kit available for the session!

Apple Makes Troubleshooting "Fun"

Apple's customer service philosophy extends to its phone support, AppleCare. One recruitment ad for an AppleCare position describes the jobs as follows: "Apple is passionate about creating the world's most innovative products. We are just as passionate about assisting the people who use them. So as an At-Home Advisor for the AppleCare Program, when customers call in with questions, you won't just provide answers, you'll provide an experience. You'll focus on the small details and be able to impress, engage, and inspire. You'll help to delight each and every one of our customers, realizing that troubleshooting can be rewarding and fun."[4]

Apple is probably the only company that describes troubleshooting as fun. The same job site had hundreds of other positions for a variety of technical repair positions. Most of the jobs required skills such as the ability to diagnose, troubleshoot, and repair defects.

Apple was the only company soliciting technical repair positions where passion was a prerequisite for the job. Apple is always thinking about the customer experience—in the store or on the phone.

Many people say that Apple stores are popular because of the quality of the products. Of course, that's partly true. If your products stink, it's going to be harder, if not impossible, to turn those products into a memorable experience. But according to Ron Johnson, "People come to the Apple Store for the experience, and they're willing to pay a premium for that. There are lots of components to that experience, but maybe the most important—and this is something that can translate to any retailer—is that the staff isn't focused on selling stuff. It's focused on building relationships and trying to make people's lives better."[5]

Your customers care about finding meaning in their lives, and oftentimes they aren't aware of how a product or service can bring out talents or abilities they didn't even know they had. Help them unleash their inner genius, and you'll create a loyal customer for life.

CHECKOUT

1. **Teach people about products.** Develop educational or instructional material to help your customers understand your products. Create an immersive experience, stimulating multiple senses. Customers should be able to see the product, hear about it, and touch it, if possible.

2. **Offer classes or tutorials.** Think about offering classes or tutorials in person or online to empower your customers and to teach them something new.

3. **Create culture-focused job descriptions.** Design a customer-focused culture starting in the job description. Clearly describe the type of person you're looking for, preferably someone who is committed to helping people live their best lives.

CHAPTER 12

Create Wow Moments

The brain remembers the emotional components of an experience better than any other aspect.

—John Medina

When Steve Jobs passed away on October 5, 2011, the world didn't just lose one of its great visionaries, but it also lost an astonishing corporate storyteller. His presentations, "Stevenotes" as they were fondly called, had all the elements of a Broadway production, including a cast, drama, heroes, villains, and props. Most people use presentations to deliver information, often dryly. Steve Jobs gave presentations that informed, educated, and entertained.

The most memorable parts of Jobs's presentations were what I call wow moments. These wow moments were carefully scripted and exhaustively rehearsed. It took an estimated 450 hours of work and rehearsals to create and deliver the twenty-minute presentation to introduce the Lion operating system in June 2011. Jobs was fanatical about each and every element of the presentation from the lighting to the messages. He knew the content of every slide, every font, and every color that was used on every slide. But nothing was more important in a presentation than the moment when the audience would gasp and say to themselves, *I need that!*

The Brain Does Not Pay Attention to Boring Things

No matter how sensational you think your product is, nobody is going to care if the message you're using to communicate the product's benefits is dry, confusing, and convoluted. Neuroscientist John Medina taught me that the brain does not pay attention to boring things. It is simply not programmed to grasp abstract concepts.

Instead he recommends creating an emotionally charged event, which is the equivalent of a mental Post-it Note for the brain. Medina says the brain's amygdala is chockful of the neurotransmitter dopamine. So when the brain detects an emotionally charged event (e.g., joy, fear, surprise), the amygdala releases dopamine into the system that greatly aids memory and information processing. Let's recall three of Jobs's emotionally charged events:

1984: The Ad and the Launch

When it came time to launch the Macintosh, the machine that revolutionized personal computers, Jobs wanted a television spot that would put a stamp on people's minds. The ad agency Chiat/Day developed the famous Big-Brother-themed "1984" ad, which ran only once during Super Bowl XVIII. More than 90 million people saw the ad, and it became the most admired television ad for the next two decades. Amazingly, the ad was nearly scrapped. When Jobs previewed the ad for the Apple board in December 1983, they hated it. Apple CEO John Sculley admitted he got cold feet. Jobs eventually won the argument, of course, but the story reminds us that Jobs intuitively understood the power of emotion in building a brand.

The 1984 television ad wasn't the only wow moment Jobs had up his sleeve. In what is still considered one of the most dramatic reveals of any product in history, Jobs introduced the Macintosh with a magician's flourish. On January 24, 1984, the Macintosh became the first computer to introduce itself. After building the audience's anticipation with a deftly crafted speech with IBM playing the narrative's antagonist, Jobs whipped the audience into a frenzy of excitement. He then walked to the center of the stage where the Macintosh had been sitting in a cloth bag on a small table. Jobs pulled out the computer, attached the keyboard and mouse, and put in a floppy disk. The theme from *Chariots of Fire* began to play, and the words *MACINTOSH INSANELY GREAT* scrolled on the screen. The graphics were unlike anything anyone had ever seen on a computer. Jobs smiled, turned to the audience, and said, "We've done a lot of talking about Macintosh, but today, for the first time, I'd like to let Macintosh speak for itself."[1] The audience gasped and cheered as they heard the computer say, *Hello, I'm Macintosh. It sure is great to get out of that bag.* Without the benefit of PowerPoint or Apple Keynote (both of which had yet to be invented), Jobs gave one of the most awe-inspiring product launches in history.

2001: 1,000 Songs in Your Pocket

The iPod began Apple's transformation from a computer company into a brand that would make devices to change the way we live, work, and play. On October 23, 2001, Jobs unveiled the iPod—a music player that came with 5 GB of storage, not a revolutionary advance in technology. But Jobs had a wow moment in his pocket, literally. He said 5 GB of storage was enough to carry 1,000 songs. Oh, and there was one more thing… 1,000 songs fit in your pocket. The size of the iPod—along with its ease of use—made it different. "I just happen to have one right here in my pocket,"[2] said Jobs as he pulled an iPod from the front pocket of his signature blue jeans.

Apple Revolutionizes the Phone

On January 9, 2007, Steve Jobs introduced the iPhone and gave what I consider his greatest presentation. As he did twenty years earlier in the Macintosh presentation, he began by building the anticipation. "Every once in a while a revolutionary product comes along that changes everything,"[3] he said. He reminded his audience that Apple had introduced the Macintosh, which revolutionized the computer industry, and the iPod that revolutionized the music industry. "Today we're launching three revolutionary products of this class," Jobs added. "The first one is a widescreen iPod with touch controls. The second is a revolutionary mobile phone. And the third is a breakthrough Internet communications device." Jobs slowly repeated each of the devices once, a second time, and a third. Finally he concluded, "Are you getting it? These are not three separate devices. This is one device, and we are calling it, iPhone!"

Steve Jobs knew how to turn a presentation into an awe-inspiring and memorable event. He was the consummate salesman, and his techniques work just as well on the sales floor as they did on the presentation stage.

Siri, What's the Weather Like Today?

Siri is the personal assistant first introduced on the iPhone 4S. Siri lets you use your voice to ask questions, send messages, schedule activities, place phones calls, and much more. Because Siri knows what you say, understands what you mean, and even talks back, it provides thousands of memorable moments at Apple Stores.

Apple senior vice president of worldwide marketing, Phil Schiller, introduced Siri on October 4, 2011. Before Schiller revealed Siri, he spent the first twenty minutes of his presentation introducing the new iPhone 4S and its improved features: graphics, gaming, photographs, and video. "It's the most amazing iPhone yet,"[4] Schiller said. "But I haven't told you the best feature." And with that Schiller introduced Siri with this Twitter-friendly headline: "Siri is your intelligent assistant that helps you get things done just by asking."

Apple's senior vice president of iPhone software, Scott Forstall, then took the stage to demonstrate Siri. He began by asking it simple questions such as, "What is the weather like today?" Siri responded by saying, "Here is the forecast for today." Then came the wow moment. Forstall wanted to demonstrate that Siri understands words and context, the meaning behind the words. "Do I need a raincoat today?" Forstall asked Siri. "It sure looks like rain today," Siri responded.

Forstall continued to demonstrate context by asking Siri to find a Greek restaurant in Palo Alto. Siri returned this response: "I found fourteen Greek restaurants. Five of them are in Palo Alto. I've sorted them by rating." Forstall concluded the demo with this question: "Who are you?" Siri responded, "I am a humble personal assistant." The audience laughed and cheered. The mental Post-it had been stuck on their brains.

Apple sales professionals demonstrating the Siri technology encourage customers to challenge the personal assistant with questions. Some of the most common questions include "What is the weather like today?" or "Where can I hide a dead body? (Siri offers a flip response to the effect that it's illegal to do that and then points you to the nearest cemetery.) But in many cases customers are challenging Siri with far more involved questions such as "What is the meaning of life?" Apple employees encourage customers to stump Siri. It becomes a game where everyone—employees and customers—is having great fun. Customers get a laugh when a Specialist will ask Siri, "Are there other smartphones?" Siri's response: "There are other smartphones?"

Some Apple Specialists will turn it into a game with a group of customers. A Specialist demonstrating Siri to one customer might notice another customer watching and encourage the second customer to participate in the fun. Pretty soon the second customer is wowed, and a third, a fourth, and so on. Siri is one example where shared wow moments have even more impact than private moments. The employee plays an important role in the narrative.

It's also important to customize wow moments for the customer. An Apple employee recently shared with me a time when he was talking to a business professional about the iPhone 4S and he encouraged the customer to ask Siri about a business project. The employee explained that Siri understands what you *say* and what you *mean*. The customer proceeded to describe a concept he had for a business. "Tell me about other companies with similar ideas," he asked Siri. The personal assistant took a couple of minutes to return a response, but it gave the customer an answer that left the man in awe. The customer probed deeper. He would ask questions such as "What are the legal ramifications?" and so on. Siri would respond, "I have what I believe is your answer," and provided a link to a legal website. Both employee and customer were pleasantly surprised.

Both were learning about Siri's capabilities at the same time. The customer had experienced a wow moment, and the employee had a new wow moment he could replicate with another customer.

If the business customer had simply picked up the phone, the sale might never have happened, because (1) he might not have considered having a conversation with the phone, and (2) he would not have thought of asking Siri business-related questions. Instead, the customer learned that Siri could be a powerful business tool but only after a well-trained employee facilitated the conversation, leading the customer to a personalized wow moment.

Ten Minutes to Resolve a Four-Year Dilemma

Connect wow moments to people's lives. One Apple employee said that in ten minutes he sold a MacBook to a customer who had spent four years considering whether he should convert from PC to Mac. The Specialist "listened" carefully to the customer's concerns (step four of the five steps of service) and heard some key words: *photos* and *children*. The Specialist launched into a true, personal story about his own experience with iPhoto, Apple's photo editing and managing software that comes installed on every Mac.

The Specialist explained that he had spent one hour on iPhoto and created a gorgeous book that he had sent to one of his daughters who could not join the family for the holidays, the first time she had spent the special occasion away. The employee explained that with iPhoto he could have the book delivered on a specific date, so he timed the delivery to land on his daughter's birthday along with a customized birthday wish. The daughter called her father in tears, the dad started crying as well, and they both shared a special moment. With one benefit and one personal story, the Specialist had created a wow moment. In less than ten minutes he had persuaded a customer to make a purchase the customer had put off for several years. It's a true story that the Specialist had used before and will use again, provided the context is appropriate. But it's important to note that the Specialist was armed with the wow moment. He had it and pulled it out when he needed it to close the sale.

> *Without launching into a multi-Tweet explanation, let me just say this: in my experience Apple Store customer service is peerless.*
> —Murphy B.

iPad Wow Moments

The iPad is perfectly suited for creating wow moments, and trained Apple employees take every opportunity to create those moments. As of this writing, there are well over 140,000 apps made for the iPad. Think of something to do—for business, pleasure, or education— and there really is an app for that. Leaving a customer in awe requires probing, listening, and observing. Here are some scenarios that have played out in Apple stores.

iPad for Business

Salesperson: Are you considering the iPad for business or pleasure?

Customer: Well, business, primarily. Although our headquarters are here in town, I'm on the road a lot meeting with clients. I also maintain our company's blog and respond to customer e-mails. We're a small company, so everyone needs to be a jack-of-all-trades.

Salesperson (probed, listened, and heard key words, *travel* and *blog*, before responding)**:** I understand. Many business professionals are finding that the iPad is a powerful tool. From manufacturing to retail to services, the iPad is transforming the way companies do business. You're a blogger, so you probably know that there are thousands of apps available for the iPad, many of which are created specifically for the platform, including a version of WordPress that allows you to create, save, publish, and schedule your posts wherever you are on the road. You can even upload images directly from your iPad. Would that be helpful?

Customer: Yes, it would be. I was out of the office four days this week, but the blog needs to be updated and right now I'm the guy who does it!

Salesperson: Congratulations on maintaining the blog. Many companies start a blog but eventually abandon it.

Customer: Oh, we have a great blog. Would you like to see it?

Salesperson: I would love to. Please show me on the iPad. (Customer shows the blog.) That is gorgeous. Nicely done. Tell me, when you were out of the office this week, did you have to access files back at the home office?

Customer: Yes, but I carry around a portable hard drive.

Salesperson: Let me show you something really cool. With the iPad I can access a remote computer with a free app called GoToMyPC. Let me show you how I have access to my home computer. (Salesperson demonstrates app.) When you get home, download the free app on your iPad, and the next time you travel, just keep your work computer on when you leave the home office and you'll have access to all your files. No need to carry around a hard drive. Everything you need for business is all right here.

For this particular businessman, remote access to his PC became the wow moment that ultimately convinced him that the iPad was a necessary device for business productivity. Note that the salesperson did not show the customer how to play Angry Birds on the iPad. Games were not contextual to the conversation, so there was no need to bring it up. Games would not have left the customer in awe. The salesperson also took the opportunity to get the customer to touch the device when he asked to see the company blog, and instead of simply describing the remote access app, the salesperson *showed* the customer how it works in the real world. Finally the salesperson began using language that assumed the customer would own an iPad (e.g., "when you get home"). This wow moment cannot happen, however, if the salesperson does not probe, listen, engage, and come prepared with examples.

FaceTime Makes a Mom's Day

Customer: My daughter thinks I need an iPod Touch. I'm not so sure. I don't listen to music or play games, so although she thinks it's cool, I'm not convinced.

Salesperson (turns to daughter): Is there a reason why you're recommending an iPod Touch for your mom? Have you considered an iPhone?

Daughter: She wouldn't use an iPhone. My mom is eighty-three years old and uses her home phone to call us.

Salesperson: Oh, do you live far away?

Daughter: Not that far, but far enough so we don't see her every day.

Salesperson: We?

Daughter: Yes, my husband and kids as well as my brother who lives in another state.

Salesperson (turning to customer)**:** If you're like my mom, you can never see your kids enough. I can visit my mom every few days, and she still doesn't think I'm spending enough time with her.

Customer: If I saw my kids once a week I'd be happy! (Daughter rolls her eyes and smiles at salesperson.)

Salesperson: Doris (salesperson would have learned customer's name early in the conversation), I'm going to show you something. Brittany (daughter), while I'm with your mom, would you go over to that phone right over there and if it rings, please answer it. Now, Doris, pick up the iPod Touch and tap the icon that says FaceTime.

At this point the salesperson has Doris FaceTime the other device. Brittany answers, and mother and daughter can see and hear each other. Doris is thrilled. As they chat away the salesperson explains FaceTime and how it works over Wi-Fi without the need for a phone plan. It was the only wow moment the customer needed. Doris walked out that day with an 8 GB $200 iPod Touch. But again, this wow moment could not have played out had the salesperson not followed the five steps of service.

Wowing My Daughters

My daughters, Josephine and Lela, were ages six and four when I brought them to an Apple Store for the first time. It was such a magical experience for all of us I'll never forget it. I even took photos of the girls playing on iPads and texted the pictures to friends. The girls enjoyed wow moments and so did their dad.

I did not intend to shop at the Apple Store on that night. It was a chilly, rainy Saturday, so the mall was especially packed. My wife and I had just taken the girls to play on the mechanical rides conveniently located next to Mrs. Fields (it didn't take a genius to figure out where to place the rides). We had finished dinner and visited another store beforehand, so I was already growing tired and was ready to leave. We walked by the Apple Store, and sure enough it was packed. I peeked in and saw a tidal wave of people coming and going. *There's no way I'm going to bring two tired kids into that place tonight*, I thought. But because Apple employees are taught to greet people at the door with a warm welcome, a friendly Apple person saw us and said, "Welcome to Apple. How can we help you today?"

"Just looking. I want to see the iPad 2, but we'll come back when it's less crazy," I said.

"It's no problem. I'll have Adam assist you right away."

I didn't even have time to say "No, thank you," before Adam, a Specialist, greeted us with a big smile, ready to create a wow moment. He led us to the iPad table and within seconds—not minutes, but *seconds*—my daughters, who had never touched an iPad before, were swiping their fingers across the device and playing with it. It reminded me of a concept I wrote about in *The Innovation Secrets of Steve Jobs*—Steve Jobs believed in eliminating clutter to make products simple and easy to use. If you can build a product so simple that a child can figure it out within seconds, you'll have a winner.

Adam was trained to create wow moments. He never touched the device. Of course, he didn't have to, since my daughters couldn't wait to start playing. What I noticed, though, was that Adam did not show me business applications or even features that might appeal to me personally. He went straight to the real decision makers in our group—my girls who are the secondary customers. "Look at that, your girls already know how to use it," Adam said. "If they like to color, they'll love 'Fairy Tale Castle Coloring Book.'" With that, Adam showed us the free app that was conveniently installed on the iPads my daughters were using. They loved it. They colored, laughed, and even showed Daddy how to use it. But Adam wasn't done. In true Steve Jobs fashion he had "one more thing."

"If you take road trips, you'll love this. You can play movies to keep the kids occupied in the backseat," Adam said. And with that, Adam opened the video app and showed us a full-screen, high-definition version of my daughter Lela's favorite Disney movie, *Tangled*. "Rapunzel!" Lela screamed in delight. Adam pointed out that an accessory was available to attach the device to the rear of the front seats. I had never thought of it. In fact we had just purchased a new car, and I was considering the idea of having a DVD player installed. But in that moment I realized that the iPad was a far better alternative.

Less than ten minutes after I had decided *not* to enter the store, I was actually thinking about buying an iPad on the spot. *I know about the wow moment. I'm supposed to be immune to this!* I thought. Never underestimate the power of emotion. We left the store without buying an iPad that night, but the conversation between me and my wife on the way home left no doubt as to what would happen next. As soon as we got into the car, my wife said, "Should we buy the 16 GB or the 32 GB model?" Wow.

> Just went to the Apple Store. Seriously, they have the best customer service anywhere. Everyone is knowledgeable. —Seth Y.

A Franchise Wows Its Customers the Apple Way

I introduced the concept of wow moments to a group of franchise owners for FRSTeam, a fabric restoration company. Insurance companies recommend FRSTeam or similar vendors when items in a client's home have been damaged by flood, fire, and other catastrophic events. In many cases homeowners who have experienced a fire believe their clothes and other items are too badly damaged to be repaired. But FRSTeam uses very advanced cleaning technology to restore severely damaged items like clothes, drapes, furniture, and so on.

On its face you wouldn't expect the "experience" to play a huge role in the success of such a franchise. After all, don't they just pick up clothes and clean them? I learned differently after my first discussion with FRSTeam president Jim Nicholas.

"Don't you just pick up the damaged goods, restore them, and return them?" I asked.

"This is a very competitive industry, so we must define ourselves by the experience we provide. Yes, it's true, anyone can show up to pick up damaged items. But insurance policyholders often judge the quality of their insurance carrier by the vendors the insurance company sends out. If a client has a satisfying experience, it will get back to the insurance company and the company will continue to hire us instead of our competitors. Positive word also spreads quickly throughout the industry."[5]

After I talked about wow moments at FRSTeam's national franchise conference, major franchisees decided to put the technique into action and develop what they call "goose-bump moments" for their customers. Here's how they did it. It starts with the most customer-facing employee, the driver who picks up the damaged articles. The driver will start with the standard questions: which items have been damaged, what is your living situation, when do you need the items returned, how do we contact you, and so on. The second set of questions sets up the goose-bump moment. Once the driver has built trust, he or she will ask a personal question: is there any one item you're the most concerned about? Nicholas and his franchisees have found that among the hundreds of articles of clothing or material that have been damaged, it's typically one or two pieces that carry the most emotional impact for the customer. It could be Grandma's quilt or a child's first soccer uniform. One piece is often more important than anything else. Once the driver knows this, the goose-bump moment is teed up. The team will work extra hard to repair that one piece and return it quickly. The stories that resulted from these goose-bump moments can really give you, well, goose bumps. Here are just a few:

- An army officer had been deployed to Iraq, and before he left, his friends threw him a party. They all signed a shirt for him, a shirt that was damaged in a house fire. A FRSTeam driver learned about the special memories it held for the family and made sure the shirt was restored to like-new condition. But there was one more thing. . . . FRSTeam put the shirt in a nice memorabilia display before returning it to the family.

- Mr. Graham's sixteen-year-old son thought he had lost his favorite item in a house fire—a St. Louis Cardinals jersey signed by a dozen players. Instead of putting the item through machines, FRSTeam employees worked through the night, hand-cleaning the jersey. The next morning the driver pulled up to where the family was staying and handed the completely restored jersey to the wide-eyed boy.

- Mrs. Merz was distraught because a Winnie the Pooh stuffed animal had been so badly damaged in a fire; it looked as though she would have to discard it. She wanted her own baby to have it. The driver made a note of the emotional attachment she had to the teddy bear. Employees cleaned it first so Mrs. Merz's baby could sleep with it the same night. Mrs. Merz cried when it was returned and even sent the franchisee a photo of the child holding the teddy bear.

These goose bump moments are now a part of the FRSTeam culture. They happen every day. But it starts by asking the question, "What can we do to create a wow moment for our customers?" It also cannot happen if management does not hire for attitude and if it isn't committed to designing a culture of trust and empowerment. For example, in another goose-bump moment for FRSTeam, a customer service rep had noticed a family portrait hanging on the wall. The fire had damaged it so badly the glass frame had actually melted onto the picture, ripping large sections out of it. It wasn't the type of article that FRSTeam typically restores, and it appeared irreparable. But the driver knew Photoshop, and *on his own time* repaired the portrait. He meticulously touched up the portrait of the four family members, replaced the glass, and returned it personally to the family.

The FRSTeam driver who repaired the photo on his own time makes $12 an hour, about the same hourly wage as people on the Apple sales floor. Don't ever make the excuse that customer service is directly tied to how much a person makes in salary or commissions. The FRSTeam driver and the typical Apple Retail employee are committed to delivering an extraordinary experience because both brands live the principles revealed in Part I. The driver doesn't see his job as simply picking up and dropping off items, and the Apple employee doesn't see his or her job as selling computers. Both have internalized the vision to rebuild lives (FRSTeam) and to enrich lives (Apple). They are also trained to engage the customer in conversations that facilitate an emotional engagement with their respective brands. Don't "sell" things to your customers. Wow them instead.

CHECKOUT

1. **Create wow moments.** Think about creating wow moments around your products or services. Apple employees know how to create such memorable moments for each product category. Customize the experience by using examples and stories relevant to the customer.

2. **Obey the ten-minute rule.** Provide a wow moment in the first ten minutes of a conversation. Research has shown that people "tune out" of a conversation after approximately ten minutes. Hook them back into the conversation.

3. **Mimic the presentation stage.** Consider the sales floor as a stage with the salesperson as the presenter and the customer as the audience. Train your staff to see themselves as presenters delivering memorable and engaging moments that leave their audiences speechless.

CHAPTER 13

Rehearse the Script

It's the intersection of technology and liberal arts that makes our hearts sing.

—Steve Jobs

On March 2, 2011, Steve Jobs introduced the iPad 2, the second generation of its pioneering tablet. The first iPad had sold 15 million units the previous year and was hailed as the most successful consumer product ever launched. Although his health was declining, Steve Jobs took the stage because as he told the audience, Apple had been working on the product for a long time and he didn't want to miss it. Although the iPad had a 90 percent market share and was one of the fastest-selling consumer products in history, Jobs had an even better model ready to roll.

The iPad 2 trumped its predecessor in three ways: thinner, lighter, faster. Those three adjectives provided the script for Jobs's presentation as well as all of Apple's marketing, advertising, and in-store materials. Jobs spent seven minutes revealing the benefits of the iPad 2 in more detail:

- **"The first thing, it's dramatically faster."** Jobs described the new A5 chip as a dual-core processor whose overall performance was twice as fast as the original iPad and ran graphics nine times faster. "A5 is quite an achievement. It's twice as fast on CPU performance, nine times faster graphics, and the first iPad was no slouch," Jobs said.[1]

- **"One of the most startling things about the iPad 2 is that it is dramatically thinner."** Jobs explained that the iPad 2 was not a little bit thinner, but one-third thinner. "It's 33 percent thinner. That's dramatic. For those of you who have an iPhone 4, the new iPad 2 is actually thinner than your iPhone 4. When you get your hands on one, it feels totally different," added Jobs.

- **"In addition to thinner, it's lighter as well."** Jobs explained that the weight of the iPad 2 was reduced from 1.5 pounds to 1.3 pounds, "You might not think that's a lot, but at 1.5 pounds, one-tenth of a pound is a lot. It feels quite a bit lighter."

The iPad 2 Script

Although it took Jobs only seven minutes to reveal the previous information, the script served as the narrative for Apple's key messages, press releases, in-store signage, television commercials, websites, and conversations on the sales floor.

- **Press Release.** Apple issued the iPad 2 press release after Jobs gave his presentation (and not a minute before). The press release was titled, "Apple Launches iPad 2: All-New Design Is Thinner, Lighter, and Faster."[2] The press release also featured the following information:

  > A new design that is 33 percent thinner and 15 percent lighter than the original iPad.

  > A new dual-core A5 processor that offers faster performance and graphics.

  > Although it is thinner, lighter, and faster, the iPad 2 delivers up to ten hours of battery life.

- **In-Store Signage.** Upon the iPad's release, in-store signs were unfurled and placed strategically near the entrance and on the walls. The signs read: "iPad 2: Thinner, Lighter, Faster."

- **Corporate Video.** The official Apple corporate video that ran on the Apple website and on YouTube highlighted the following features of the iPad 2: one-third thinner, 15 percent lighter, all new dual-core A5 chip with nine times the graphic performance, and ten hours of battery life.

- **Television Commercial.** Apple created a television commercial for the iPad 2 titled, "We Believe." "This is what we believe,"[3] a narrator began, "Technology alone is not enough. Faster, thinner, lighter, those are all good things. But when technology gets out of the way, everything becomes more delightful, even magical... that's when you end up with something like this." The name "iPad 2" was never mentioned in the commercial. The name of the product only showed up on screen at the end.

Creating a script, crafting a compelling narrative, and sticking to it resulted in millions of conversations echoing the key messages "thinner, lighter, faster." Following are some samples of the headlines from major blogs and newspapers that ran after the iPad 2 introduction.

- iPad 2: Thinner, Lighter, Faster—*USA Today*

- iPad 2: Thinner, Lighter, Faster Transforms the Experience—MacDailyNews

- iPad 2: All New Design Is Thinner, Lighter & Faster—Endgadget

- iPad 2: Thinner, Lighter, Faster—*Good Housekeeping*

- A Great Tablet Made Thinner, Lighter, and Faster—CNET

When I walked into an Apple Store after the iPad 2 went on sale, the Specialist had internalized the product's messages and delivered them perfectly. "Why is this model better than the original?"

I asked. "It's better for several reasons," said the Specialist. "The processor is faster than the original, and it's really noticeable when you're playing games. It's a lot thinner. In fact, it's 33 percent thinner. That's dramatic. And lighter. Go ahead, pick it up and see for yourself."

One Apple Store employee told me that reviewing and rehearsing the script was one of the most important concepts he learned from my book *The Presentation Secrets of Steve Jobs*. The script comes from the top. Key messages will be created at Apple headquarters in Cupertino and delivered publicly by the CEO or one of the division leaders. The announcement will be followed by press releases, marketing, advertising, and in-store material. The message customers hear on the sales floor should be no different. Employees have the flexibility to personalize the messages, but the key benefits behind each product remain consistent.

The Twitter-Friendly Headline

Apple CEO Tim Cook follows the same process as Jobs did. What's the iPhone 4S? According to Cook on October 4, 2011, "The iPhone 4S is our most amazing iPhone yet."[4] The Apple press release for the same day read: "Apple today announced iPhone 4S, the most amazing iPhone yet." The front page of the Apple website featured only one product, the iPhone 4S. The copy read: "It's the most amazing iPhone yet." Apple created a television commercial for the phone highlighting Siri, the personal assistant. The commercial ended with the words, "Say hello to the most amazing iPhone yet."

You might have noticed something about both the phrases used to describe the iPad 2 and the iPhone 4S. Both are short enough to fit well within a Twitter post of 140 characters. Simple messages are more easily processed by the brain. Simple is more memorable and easier for employees to repeat to customers. Apple makes sure its key messages are concise, typically one short sentence. Although Apple doesn't purposely use Twitter as its test, it's uncanny how every product description as far back as 2001 can fit easily within a Twitter post:

iPod: 1,000 songs in your pocket.

MacBook Air: The world's thinnest notebook.

iPhone: Apple reinvents the phone.

iPad: A magical and revolutionary device.

iCloud: Stores your content and wirelessly pushes it to all your devices.

An Apple-like approach to the marketing and sales conversation starts with developing key messages about your service, product, company, or cause. The Twitter-friendly headline—the overarching key message—should be no more than one sentence and 140 characters in length. When the company Reckitt Benckiser, which makes products like Calgon, Lysol, and Woolite, introduced a new Clearasil face-wash dispenser, its executive director stated publicly that the campaign was modeled on Apple. That meant creating one key message that would be repeated in YouTube videos, commercials, and other marketing channels. The repeatable key message in the Clearasil campaign was, "The perfect dose for visibly clear skin" (thirty-nine characters). When Facebook founder Mark Zuckerberg introduced a new look for his site's homepage called Timeline, he said, "Timeline is the whole story of your life on a single page" (fifty-seven characters). It was memorable, and yes, many observers compared Zuckerberg to Steve Jobs. The Timeline description turned up in thousands of blogs and news articles. Zuckerberg had succeeded in concisely framing the narrative. Steve Jobs, who gave Zuckerberg business advice, would have been proud.

> *In Apple Store Oxford Circus. Always amazed at how the staff are so expert, friendly, and charming.* —Breffni W.

The Message Map

I could spend the rest of this chapter giving you more examples of effective scripts, but it won't do you much good unless you can

162 THE APPLE EXPERIENCE

implement the technique for yourself. So here goes. I'm about to introduce you to a powerful and effective communications technique that will help you create your own script and to share the script with your team and your customers. It's called the *message map*: a one-page visual depiction of your story.

The message map is stunningly effective. One client of mine—a global wireless brand—laminated its final message map and would simply pass it across the table to potential customers in face-to-face conversations. I nearly passed out when I heard it, because the message map is meant to be kept internal and to be used to create presentations, ads, and marketing material. But my clients reassured me when they said, "It worked fine. In fact, it helped us win several multimillion-dollar accounts!" Following are the steps you need to create your own message map:

1. Create a Twitter-friendly headline. You should be able to describe your service or product in 140 characters or less. Before Twitter there were the Google guys, Sergey Brin and Larry Page. They intuitively understood the importance of this exercise. When Brin and Page were looking for funding, they pitched Google to investors at Sequoia Capital. One investor told me that the investors "got it" in one sentence: "Google provides access to the world's information in one click" (sixty-two characters). The description was so persuasive that the investors now demand a one-sentence pitch from any entrepreneur seeking funding for a company or product. Keep your headline concise, specific, and descriptive. Above all, make sure it does not exceed 140 characters.

2. Create three or at most four supporting points. In short-term memory, people can only recall about three or four pieces of content. Cram too many message points in your narrative, and it will run off the page. In some cases your Twitter-friendly headline can preview the supporting messages. For example, the iPad 2 was "thinner, lighter, and faster." It works as a headline and fills out the rest of the message map.

3. Develop three or four details for each of your supporting messages. These details should include data, stories, and examples.

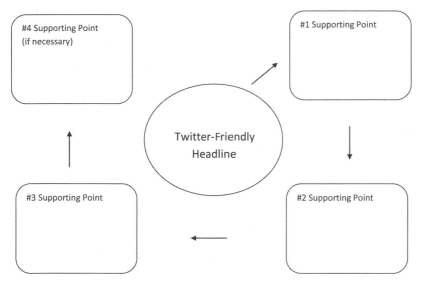

Figure 13.1 Message Map Template

4. Cut-and-paste the content you developed in the first three steps into the four to five bubbles of a message map template (Figure 13.1). A template like the one in Figure 13.1 can be created by using Microsoft Word or Pages for Mac; it can also be created using Microsoft PowerPoint or Apple Keynote software.

To show you how to apply these four steps, Table 13.1 shows how Apple could have created a message map for the iPhone 4S.

Figure 13.2 shows step four—all the content from the first three steps listed in Table 13.1 positioned in the appropriate place on the message map for the iPhone 4S.

And there you have it. Message mapping is one of the most powerful communication techniques you will ever find. A message map can provide the foundation for a thirty-second elevator pitch, a ten-minute conversation, or a twenty-minute presentation. Best of all, every member of your sales staff can speak from the same playbook. Keep in mind that every spokesperson for the brand should be encouraged and given the flexibility to use different examples and stories that mean something to him or her and that are relevant to his or her customers.

Table 13.1 Message Map Steps One to Three for Apple iPhone 4S

Step One (Headline)	Step Two (Supporting Points)	Step Three (Sub-Supporting Points)
The most amazing iPhone yet.	1. Dual-core A5 chip	• 2× faster performance • 7× faster graphics • Games look fantastic
	2. All new camera	• 8 megapixels • Full 1080p HD video recording • A true replacement for most point-and-shoot cameras
	3. iOS 5 and iCloud	• Notification center • iMessage • 200 new features • Store your content and push it to all your devices
	4. Siri	• Your personal assistant • Use your voice to send messages, ask questions, get information • Siri understands what you say and *mean*

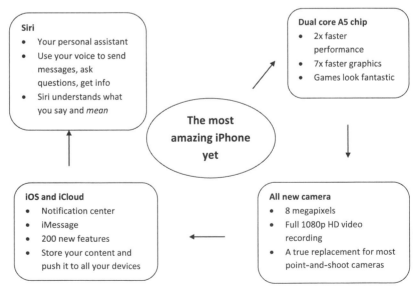

Figure 13.2 Complete Message Map for iPhone 4S

Creating a Brand Message Map

If your company carries only a few products like Apple (Macs, iPods, iPads), then you should have a message for each product or at least each product category. But what if your brand carries hundreds of products like the soap company Lush? The brand does spend a lot of money sending new products to the homes of its employees so they can talk about the products from personal knowledge, but it would be impossible—and unpractical—to create a message map about each bar of soap. So in a case like Lush, the company could create a message map to share its brand and core values—a messaging template that would apply to every product in the store. Figure 13.3 shows what a message map could look like for values that the Lush brand represents.

This message map has only three key points that reinforce the headline. Three is a good number. Four is acceptable, but try to avoid creating a message map with more than four supporting

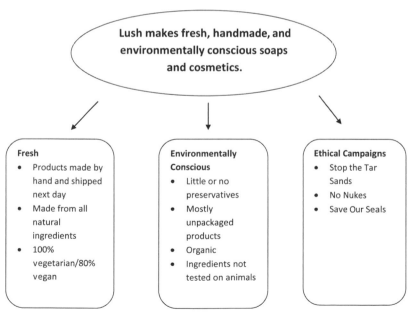

Figure 13.3 Brand Message Map for Lush

messages. Make it easy for all brand spokespeople to remember and deliver the story.

In Chapter 8 we revealed the Apple five steps of service. Step three is to "present a solution." The solution includes a clear description of the benefits. It answers the question, "What product is right for me, and why should I care?" You and your staff will have a hard time explaining those solutions clearly and persuasively without a script. Rehearsing a script does not imply that your employees must stick to a predetermined template (that's why car salesmen and phone solicitors annoy us so much). But it does mean that everyone—every customer facing employee—knows the key messages, internalizes the narrative, and delivers the story consistently.

CHECKOUT

1. **Script a story.** Make sure that every product, service, or program has a story—narrative—that has been scripted for it. The script must use clear, simple language that is repeatable and memorable.

2. **Create a message map.** Make a message map for the product, service, or company. You can use a small team of people to help you craft it, but be careful about circulating the message map among too many people to get their buy-in. The goal is to have just the right amount of content that can fit easily on one page. Too many points defeat the purpose.

3. **Share the message map.** Circulate the message map, and coach the team to repeat the key messages. Everyone in a position to discuss the product should have at least three or four key messages ready to deliver and a story or example to accompany each message. If they don't get to each message in every conversation, that's OK. It's more important that they are armed with the story when they need it.

CHAPTER 14

Deliver a Consistent Experience

*Be a yardstick of quality. Some
people aren't used to an environment
where excellence is expected.*

—Steve Jobs

On the days following the passing of Steve Jobs, the clean and uncluttered glass windows that are a hallmark of Apple Stores were suddenly filled with sticky notes from millions of people around the world who left handwritten expressions of sympathy. Nearly every one of the 360 Apple Stores became makeshift shrines to the visionary leader:

Toronto: "Thank you, Steve."

San Francisco: "iSad"

London: "Steve, you were the role model for our generation."

Hong Kong: "Steve, thanks for pursuing what you wanted to do in life."

China: "The one and only Steve Jobs, remembered forever."

Japan: "You're a genius, a legend, a fighter, and my hero."

At the Apple Store in Tokyo's Ginza district, a woman placed a bouquet in front of the store, backed away, and stood silently in prayer. Dozens of flowers had already been placed on the ground. Personal sentiments such as, "Steve, thank you for your genius," were left behind. People even left red apples carved to show a depiction of Steve Jobs. Other apples simply had a bite taken out of them to mimic the iconic Apple logo.[1]

As I watched this display of emotion on YouTube clips that people had uploaded from around the world, I thought, "How could one man inspire such a show of affection from millions of people who never met him?" The former president of The Ritz-Carlton, Simon Cooper, once told me that people never fall in love with a thing. They fall in love with people who make them feel special. The mourners who were laying flowers in front of Apple Stores had lost someone who had created an experience that made them feel special, and they chose to display their emotion at a symbol of that experience—the Apple Retail Store. People may enjoy their

Mourners in China. *Source: Getty Images*

iPods or iPads, but nobody is going to spontaneously write a note or lay flowers in front of a store because they like its products. Yes, those people were honoring Steve's legacy, but the location in which they chose to display their emotions carries a special place in their memories.

People are the heart of an Apple Retail Store, and the heart beats consistently from store to store. If you step into the Apple Store in Tokyo or Paris, you'll meet friendly people who are committed to creating an empowering and enriching experience for each and every customer. Visit an Apple Store in San Francisco or Hong Kong, and you'll meet Geniuses who don't fix computers but repair relationships instead. And whether you buy a Mac in Manhattan or Madrid, you will be introduced to Creatives who empower customers to find solutions for themselves.

In every store, "the staff is exceptionally well trained, and they're not on commission, so it makes no difference to them if they sell you an expensive new computer or help you make your old one run better so you're happy with it. Their job is to figure out what you need and help you get it, even if it's a product Apple doesn't carry,"[2] said Ron Johnson. "Compare that with other retailers where the emphasis is on cross-selling and upselling and basically, encouraging customers to buy more, even if they don't want or need it. That doesn't enrich their lives, and it doesn't deepen the retailer's relationship with them. It just makes their wallets lighter." Regardless of which Apple Store you visit, you will find:

- Friendly people who follow the Apple five steps of service, beginning with a warm welcome as soon as you step through the door

- Employees positioned at the front entrance during new product launches so they can cheer and clap for customers when they walk out with their new devices

- Smiling staff who distribute bottled water or pizza slices to people in line during the aforementioned product launches. Some even hand out umbrellas on rainy days

- Sales associates who complete transactions with iPod Touches equipped with credit card readers

- Interactive areas where kids can play with computers loaded with games and educational software

- One to One training tables where Creatives teach customers to use Apple products and software

- Genius Bars where highly trained employees troubleshoot concerns or malfunctioning products

- Personalized setup areas where Apple employees provide customers with assistance in getting their new devices up and running. The setup provides customers with an incentive to buy products in the Apple Store, and it also reduces problems when people get home. It also reduces frustration. Setup issues are the most common reasons for visits to the Genius Bar.

Customers will pay a premium for excellent service and for the consistent delivery of that service. In one survey, nearly 75 percent of customers said that businesses do not value their customers enough.[3] They also said they are willing to pay a 10 percent premium for excellent customer service. I agree. In 1996, I bought my wife's engagement ring from Tiffany & Co., knowing full well that I was paying a premium for its Fifth Avenue location, its quality, and for the joy of seeing her face light up when she saw the blue box. But it was the service that ultimately sold me.

When I got engaged, I was working for CNN in New York City, living in a small, 700-square-foot, studio apartment. I didn't trust leaving the ring there for the two months before I flew back to California where I had planned to pop the question. "No problem," said the friendly Tiffany clerk. "We can keep it here in our vault until you're ready to pick it up." I was also told that my wife could walk into any Tiffany store anywhere in the world and get it cleaned as she waited—no fees or the hassle of having to come back later to retrieve the ring. The clerk wasn't exaggerating. To this day, my wife and I drop into a Tiffany store from time to time and wait for a few minutes while they clean her ring. They instantly recognize the Tiffany design and treat us like royalty—*in every store, every time.* The treatment she gets is far more rewarding than if she just took her ring to another jeweler or jewelry repair location. Tiffany's quality enticed me, but the consistency of the experience won me over and created a customer for life. Apple has followed the same philosophy to become the crown jewel of the retail world.

Training a Genius to Fix Relationships

No two geniuses are exactly alike, but at Apple they all receive the same intensive training at Apple's Cupertino headquarters. When Apple customers have a problem or need a repair, they are asked to make an appointment at the Genius Bar, where someone with exceptionally high technical skills will troubleshoot iPads, iPods, Macs, or iPhones. The Genius Bar was actually Ron Johnson's idea. You might recall from Part I that the Four Seasons Hotels inspired the Apple Store customer service philosophy. That prompted Johnson to send his first store managers to explore luxury hotels like Four Seasons and The Ritz-Carlton. Johnson approached Jobs and suggested they create something in between a concierge and a bar and staff it with the smartest Mac experts. They could call them Geniuses. Jobs immediately dismissed the idea, but Johnson learned the very next day that Jobs had trademarked the name *Genius Bar.* Johnson fearlessly made his case, and it worked.

Apple keeps a tight lid on its policies, techniques, and what employees can and cannot say publicly. But it keeps an especially tight rein on Geniuses. Very few Geniuses have spoken publicly. Those who have spoken have revealed that each Genius goes through two weeks of intensive training and a battery of certifications at Apple headquarters. The training includes role-playing in an Apple Store mock-up.

According to confidential Apple training manuals published in the *Wall Street Journal,* once the training is over, there's very little they don't know about Apple products and they are all trained to offer emergency aid for emotionally distraught customers. One excerpt from the manual detailed how Geniuses at every store, in every country, and in every language should handle distraught customers who bring in broken devices or who fear they have lost all their data. According to the manual, Geniuses should do the following:

- Look for the underlying cause of the person's reaction. Is it frustration, fear, confusion?[4]
- Reassure the customer that you are here to help.
- Listen and limit your responses to simple reassurances that you are doing so (e.g., "Uh-huh" and "I understand").
- Apologize when appropriate (e.g., "On behalf of Apple I would like to apologize...").
- Take notes. Even when people are venting, they are often providing important details. It will save time later and help you listen without interrupting.
- Acknowledge the customer's underlying reaction. "I can certainly understand how frustrating this can be." "I know this can seem very confusing."

Inconsistency destroys a brand's value. Every time a customer interacts with your brand—on the web, on the phone, or in the store—that customer is judging the experience. An inconsistent experience could spell disaster for any brand. Apple doesn't take any customer touchpoint for granted. Every experience in the store—whether it happens in the "red zone" (sales floor) or at the Genius Bar—is planned and practiced down to the exact conversation. The result is that customers *should* get a consistent experience in any store, in any language, each and every time. I say *should* because, as we've discussed, it doesn't always happen. But it happens consistently enough to make Apple one of the world's premier retailers.

Branding experts will tell you that consistency of experience is one of the main components for building a lasting brand. For this to happen, though, every employee must be made responsible for creating and delivering the experience and fulfilling the brand promise. "Merely explaining and communicating the experience to employees will not differentiate an organization from its competitors. Successful organizations need to embed the experience into the corporate culture, hiring criteria, education programs, employee objectives, compensation plans, and incentive programs,"[5] according to customer service expert Lior Arussy. "As consumers, we seek to do business with companies that are constantly elevating the quality and consistency of their customer experiences. We want to deal with empowered employees who not only have the tools and authority to solve our challenges, but the knowledge and background to truly understand our challenges and how we perceive and appreciate value."

Arussy believes that exceptional performance is the new standard, and every leader and employee must meet those standards and demonstrate the brand's values to establish emotional connections that each and every customer will remember and cherish. Apple is not alone in delivering a consistent experience. It lives in a rare orbit, of course, but I've studied several other brands that exist in the same galaxy. Two brands share many similarities with Apple even though they are in completely different product categories—soap and shoes.

Happy People Selling Happy Soap

At Lush, happy people make happy soap, literally—the handcrafted cosmetics are fresh, free of preservatives, and made with ingredients not tested on animals. I know because employees consistently tell me the same story over and over (recall the sample message map based on Lush talking points in Chapter 13).

The lesson of how Lush cosmetics grew from one small store in Poole, England, to a worldwide chain of 700 shops in forty-four countries holds four valuable insights for any business seeking to provide an Apple-like customer experience.

Stay True to Your Values

"We pride ourselves on ethics,"[6] according to Lush North America president Mark Wolverton, whom I interviewed for a Forbes.com column. "As we grow, we refuse to change the very things that make us unique." Wolverton told me that Lush has always strived to make a positive environmental impact. It does so by sourcing from vendors who use no child labor or animal-tested products. The products are 100 percent vegetarian and 80 percent vegan. According to Wolverton, this is the "ethical choice" that Lush has made since its inception.

Regardless of the choices and values you choose to make in your business, it's important to maintain a unique identity. Ask yourself, what does my company stand for? Apple is in the business of enriching lives. What business are you in?

Communicate Your Values

Once you know what your company stands for, you must communicate your unique values through multiple channels. Individual Lush stores maintain their own Facebook pages, and Lush tells its story through its website and a free in-store newspaper called the *Lush Times*. Lush also does something unique—it gets involved in environmental causes by holding events and protests at its stores. In North America, Lush has run controversial campaigns tackling issues like overpackaging in the cosmetics industry, the Canadian commercial seal hunt, and the Canadian oil sands (the extraction of oil from Alberta's tar sands has sparked fierce environmental opposition). To raise awareness of such issues, Lush staff at some stores have stripped down to nothing but an apron to protest overpackaging, storefronts have been converted into giant blood-spattered placards, and protests have been held to end Canada's tar sands project and encourage investment in clean energy.

Wolverton acknowledged that Lush's tactics might turn off some customers. (Lush has stores in Alberta, and some employees have family members who work in the oil sands.) But they are also passionate about their values and communicating those values. "We strive for a substantial amount of transparency in the business. We must act in a green fashion and the causes we support. It all fits together," says Wolverton.

You might disagree with Lush's stand on environmental issues—and many do—but the store has values and sticks to them. It's more important that as a business you stand for something and communicate those values consistently.

Involve Employees

Lush includes its employees in every facet of its business—from the causes it supports to the discussion of its products. Again, Lush does something unique. It sends new products to every employee's home so they can use it for themselves. Employees are the brand's best ambassadors, so this intimate knowledge of each and every new product carries over to a high rate of customer satisfaction and loyalty. I visited four stores (Orlando, Carmel, San Francisco, and Paris) and in each location, the employees had thorough knowledge of every product—from soaps to shampoos. Lush has thousands of employees who know the details of every product. I've visited many small businesses with far fewer employees who don't know very much about the products or services. There's no excuse for poor training. Apple, too, involves its employees in the success of the company. Apple managers are frequently challenging Specialists to come up with radical ideas to improve the customer experience. Although an employee on the Apple sales floor cannot reposition product or alter the visual standard of the store handed down by Apple headquarters, they do have flexibility to make decisions to improve the customer experience. For example, employees are designated in zones (iPad table, MacBook table, etc.). If, however, an employee in the iPad section notices that a customer has been standing for a while in the iPod section and looks confused, that employee can move to the iPod zone with no fear of reprimand from a manager.

Hire for Cultural Fit

Wolverton says Lush strives to hire people who don't see it as a job but as a lifestyle choice. "It's nice to work for a business you believe in," says Wolverton. "They are working at a job where the values behind our brand and the product fit with the choices they make in their personal lives." Apple, too, celebrates diversity. It doesn't matter if an employee wishes to sport a tattoo, pierce his body, or wear a mohawk. The customer experience is the only thing that matters. Lush's strong growth proves that you can win in business by creating an environment where people have an opportunity to grow, be involved in the business, and connect with its values. Above all, Lush teaches small business owners that it's not enough to sell a product. Sell a story as well.

Delivering Happiness One Shoe at a Time

As a business model, Zappos is simple to understand. It sells shoes, clothes, and merchandise online. But aren't there millions of sites that sell goods online? Well, they do, but not nearly as successfully as Zappos. In ten years, Zappos, which started in the San Francisco apartment of its CEO, Tony Hsieh, grew from no sales to more than one billion in gross annual sales. In 2009, Amazon purchased Zappos for $1.2 billion. Today Zappos is considered one of the best places to work as well as a champion of exceptional customer service. I have interviewed CEO Tony Hsieh before, and when I visited the Zappos headquarters in Henderson, Nevada, I had a chance to speak to many of his employees. It gave me an inside look into how Zappos has established itself as one of the leaders in customer service. Here are four tips I learned from Hsieh about building a consistent corporate culture where everybody lives the brand's values.[7]

Treat Everyone Like Family

You might remember the story I told in Part I about the shuttle bus driver who picked me up from the hotel. I was the only one on the bus. When I asked the driver why she drove all the way out to pick me up, she said, "We treat all of our customers as family. If you had a family member in town, wouldn't you pick them from their hotel or the airport?" Once I entered Zappos headquarters, I discovered that each and every employee and phone representative shared the same enthusiasm. They were eager to share their culture and would answer any question that I asked. No public relations person escorted me through the halls as they do in most companies. I could speak to anybody about anything. That's how much Zappos trusts its employees to articulate the company's vision.

Empower Your Team

The Zappos customer service reps are not required to follow a script nor do they have to adhere to time limits on their calls. Their only mission is to wow customers and create an emotional connection with them. For example, every employee has postcards sitting next to the phone. They are encouraged to build relationships with customers and drop them a handwritten note. These are simple gestures that guarantee a customer for life. Customer service isn't brain surgery. It is simply common sense, courtesy, and the desire to treat everyone—customers, partners, and employees—like family. Empower your staff to meet and exceed your customer's expectations in each and every interaction.

Share Everything

All information is shared daily with employees—average call times, sales, profits, and so on. In fact, Zappos is so open with their performance information that they post it on a board for all to see, employees and outsiders. Even during my tour I was completely free to take photographs and video. Zappos even streams its staff meetings on the Internet for anyone to see. This demonstrates a remarkable trust in their employees and a commitment to open and honest communications.

Have Fun!

During our tour, an employee interrupted our tour guide to tape some segments for the company blog. Everyone was cheering and high-fiving each other. They have parties and events, and they're encouraged to celebrate their uniqueness by decorating their cubicles—the more outrageous the better. I have never seen a group of people who have so much fun with each other. At Zappos, "fun" only becomes a problem when employees are not having it.

Tony Hsieh told me that he is not in the business of selling shoes. He's in the business of "delivering happiness." You see, although Zappos sells merchandise online, that's not what the company stands for.

Zappos is not in the business of selling shoes, just as Apple is not in the business of selling computers. It enriches lives instead. Ask yourself, "What am I really selling, and what does our company culture say about our brand? Above all, commit yourself to celebrating your culture and communicating those values across the entire organization each and every day, consistently.

CHECKOUT

1. **Communicate a bold vision.** Commit to outperforming your competitors in the area of customer service with each and every conversation and transaction. Communicate this vision consistently to your team. Consider aspirational visions like "enriching lives" or, as in the case of Zappos, to "deliver happiness." The vision you set will put forces in motion, but the quality of the vision will ultimately decide your success.

2. **Visit a Lush store, or place a phone order with Zappos.** Notice how every employee lives the brand's culture and values. Better yet, schedule an in-person tour of the Zappos headquarters next time you are in Henderson, Nevada. They welcome visitors!

3. **Hold regular meetings to reinforce your company values.** Quarterly meetings are not enough. AT&T Retail holds training sessions once a week. The Ritz-Carlton holds meetings for each department every single day. Managers in Apple Stores are reinforcing the brand's principles every shift as well. Providing superior customer service requires constant reinforcement and modeling from the top.

SETTING
THE STAGE

Most of the news articles that have tried to explain Apple's success in retail highlight the spacious, clean, and well-lit physical appearance of the stores themselves. These are all important success factors and will be addressed in this section. But please remember this: if you have not mastered the principles in Parts I and II, nothing in this section will matter.

Cosmetic changes don't matter if you have people who don't like their boss, don't like their job, and can't communicate with their customers. I decided to return to a hotel for a second time even though I didn't enjoy my first experience. It was pricey, dated, and dirty. Most of the staffers were also unfriendly. I stayed again for only one reason—it was the closest hotel to the place where I had to be the next morning and I would be arriving late the night before. When I walked in, I noticed something new. The hotel had recently added a signature scent, which seems to be a trend among some hotel chains. The Westin hotels have a signature scent, but they also provide a nice experience to complement the scent. That was the problem with my hotel. The scent was nice, but the staff was still unfriendly, the hotel was dated, and the rooms were still dirty! On a trip to Las Vegas we stayed at a beautiful smoke-free boutique hotel called Vdara. It, too, had a signature scent. The scent was so nice I actually bought the scent sticks to put in my office. But the scent was simply a bonus that capped a memorable experience.

The scent didn't make the experience—the people made the experience. But the scent reminded me of the experience.

I hesitate to use the hackneyed expression "It's like putting lipstick on a pig." But in this case it works. No amount of lipstick is going to make up for unfriendly people delivering poor service. But if you have the people and the communication right, poor packaging will actually detract from the experience you worked so hard to achieve. Ron Johnson said all great customer service experiences start with great products and a clearly defined and concise vision. Once you have the products in place, the vision, the people, and the communication, it's time to pay attention to the details of design and packaging to create a place where people feel comfortable returning again and again.

CHAPTER 15

Eliminate the Clutter

*Get rid of the crappy stuff and focus
on the good stuff.*
—Steve Jobs

W alk into an AT&T retail store in North America and you will notice that the stores have an open feel: uncluttered and spacious. Visit a Tesla electric car dealership and you will notice a similar store layout—uncluttered glass windows, simple furniture, interactive displays, and plenty of space to wander. Both brands copied Apple and are proud of it. Steve Jobs would pick up the phone and call AT&T's head of retail to offer advice on store design, and Tesla's vice president of sales and the "ownership experience," George Blankenship, sat four offices from Steve Jobs in Cupertino, California, while he worked in the retail division of Apple. There's a reason why Tesla dealerships look like Apple, feel like Apple, and are located in malls like Apple instead of traditional car lots off the beaten path. Blankenship wanted it that way. It worked for Apple and he believes it will work for Tesla because both brands must get people to "think differently" about the product—Tesla in the electric car category and Apple in 2001 when its market share was only 3 percent.

Apple changed the face of retail with its minimalist store design, open spaces, simple display tables, and large glass entrances. In doing so, it inspired other retailers including its competitor, Microsoft. As of this writing, Microsoft had opened fourteen stores around the United States and it most certainly took a page or two, or three, from the Apple Retail playbook. Friendly employees in brightly colored shirts greet visitors in stores that are spacious, clean, and uncluttered. Expansive windows invite shoppers to see the excitement inside the store and interactive display areas encourage customers to play with Microsoft products. The resemblance to the Apple Store design is more than a coincidence. The technology blog Gizmodo reported that Microsoft hired at least one Apple Store designer to act as a consultant on the new store design.

You can't blame Microsoft. A store could do worse than copying one of the greatest models in retail history. Apple has learned that its customers like open spaces, glass entrances and staircases, and simple, handcrafted oak tables. According to Apple designer Jonathan Ive, "We are absolutely consumed by trying to develop a solution that is very simple because as physical beings we understand

Grand Central Apple Store. *Source: Getty Images*

clarity."[1] Ive was speaking about product design but this philosophy extends to the design of the Apple Store as well. Nowhere is that philosophy more evident than in Apple's Grand Central Terminal store, which opened in December 2011.

The store that Apple opened in one of the world's busiest train stations, Grand Central, is radically different that most retail spaces anywhere in the world. It's notable for the lack of a retail space. You never enter a store or leave the station. There are no walls and no separation between the station and the store. No product boxes can be seen. Instead all the devices are turned on and sit on large wooden tables evenly spaced between large aisles. One observer said the store combines the elements of a hands-on science museum with an art gallery. Fine art requires open space to be seen and appreciated.

> The Grand Central Apple Store is the coolest Apple Store I've ever been in.   —Brandon E.

In Apple's world, anything that detracts from the user experience is eliminated, in product or store design. When Steve Jobs returned to Apple in 1997 he axed more than 70 percent of the products to focus on the 30 percent that were gems. "If you go out and ask people what's wrong with computers today, they'll tell you they're really complicated,"[2] said Steve Jobs in 1999 when Apple introduced the iMac. "They [computers] have a zillion cables coming out of the back, they're really big and noisy, they're really ugly, and they take forever to get on the Internet. We set out to fix those problems."

Jobs once said that there is a strong DNA in the Apple culture to make state-of-the-art technology that people find easy to use. The DNA extends to the in-store experience. In fact, the stores embody the Apple brand, mirroring the experience of using Apple products. When the first Apple Store opened in Tysons Corner, Virginia, Jobs proudly said that Apple's entire product line was on display in the first 25 percent of the store space. There's only one button on the front of an iPad, making it so simple that a two-year-old can use it. The same design approach is evident in all of Apple's products because Steve Jobs wanted it that way. But when Jobs first applied the philosophy to the store experience he was met with very public criticism. Here's a sample:

- "Sorry, Steve, here's why Apple Stores won't work."[3]—*Businessweek*

- "Apple's problem is it still believes the way to grow is serving caviar in a world that seems pretty content with cheese and crackers."[4]—Joseph Graziano

- "I give them two years before they're turning out the lights on a very painful and expensive mistake."[5]—David Goldstein

Ten years later there were 350 Apple Stores with an aggressive roadmap for international expansion. The average location made an annual per store revenue of $34 million and made more per square foot than most luxury retailers. Now you know why Jobs avoided focus groups. He didn't believe that people knew what they wanted until he showed it to them. In many ways he was right. Many people wouldn't think about it at the time but they did, indeed, crave simplicity and space in their physical environments.

Jobs intuitively understood what neuroscientists would later find through electroencephalograph (EEG) and magnetic resonance image (MRI) brain scans. According to Dr. A. K. Pradeep, who founded Berkeley, California–based NeuroFocus, a neurological testing firm for consumer behavior, "Memory processing is influenced by suppressing distractions. Don't overwhelm the brain, forcing it to expend more energy."[6]

Pradeep argues that eliminating distractions applies to the physical in-store experience as well as the way messages are delivered. "Keep the message obvious and direct, and keep the copy and images clean and uncluttered. Let the message 'breathe' with some white space around it. And avoid the impulse to load up messages with sounds, running screens, and quick animation." Pradeep is one of the world's leading neuromarketing researchers, pioneering the application of neuroscience in marketing, advertising, and messaging. Pradeep concludes from his research that simplicity improves the shopping experience in every aspect. "Finding additional information, streamlining the purchase experience, transporting products to your home, opening the package, or fixing a problem, simplicity must be a core component of the consumer's experience."[7]

Complexity Simplified

When the Apple Store celebrated its tenth anniversary, a site called Visual Merchandising and Store Design (vmsd.com) asked a group of design experts for their thoughts on Apple Store design. Most pointed to the simple, uncluttered feel of the store as one of the primary reasons Apple revolutionized store design.[8]

- "Apple has redefined 'easy.' Nothing about shopping there is unpleasant, unattractive, or annoying."—Jan Tribbey, Victoria's Secret

- "An über-clean, fresh world."—Tom Beebe, consultant

- "They simplified retail to the point where it's you, the product, and someone who can help you."—Lee Peterson, WD Partners

- "A clean and simple environment, easy to navigate and offering ample space to experience the product and conduct meaningful conversations."—Jason Floyd, GameStop

- "Did someone say 'less is more'? Must have been Steve Jobs. Apple has mastered complexity simplified."—Stephanie Picone, IZOD Retail

One retail consultant said he cannot think of a client in ten years who has not referenced Apple as a model for reinventing the customer experience.

No Smudges Allowed

Eliminating clutter also means keeping things clean. It's not uncommon to see an employee cleaning the screen of an iPad after it gets a few smudge marks. "If you've ever been to an Apple Store opening, you'll know how meticulous they are about cleaning the windows, the floors, the shelving, and so on," says Apple blogger Gary Allen.[9] "It's almost to the point of being absurd. During the Palo Alto opening, they almost continuously cleaned the windows (inside and out) between 6:00 p.m. and 11:00 p.m. and then returned at 6:00 a.m. to start all over again. The same activity has occurred at subsequent openings. The cleaning crew must be the hardest-working team at an Apple store!"

Why is Apple different? Apple cares about things other businesses don't. It cares about elegance, space, and simplicity. It cares about smudges. Most people simply don't care about this as much as Apple, and that's the difference.

There's a restaurant near my office that is conveniently located and offers a decent selection of everything from pizza to salads. It also has coffee, beer, and wine. The problem is that it's smelly, cluttered, and messy. The kitchen has a passing grade from the health inspector, so I assume the food won't make me sick. But it leaves a bad impression for several reasons. First, the glass is never clean. There are smudges all over the front windows, the dessert tray, and even on the wine glass when I ordered a Chardonnay that was served so lightly chilled it was almost room temperature. Second, it's dusty. The fake plants, coffee bean displays, and windowsills are coated with a week's (or longer) layer of dust. Third, it's cluttered. The short walkway separating the front of the restaurant from the back room where more tables are located also acts as a storage closet. A diner has to maneuver past mops, buckets, and empty boxes.

Finally, *nobody cares*, not even the owner (which explains everything). On one occasion a large party of ten people had just left, and there were dirty dishes and glasses covering a table in the middle of the room. Right next to the table, the owner was meeting with a vendor, and I was close enough to overhear the conversation. The owner was trying to get the vendor to shave a few cents on takeout cups and packages, and he paid no attention to the mess right next to him. Forty-five minutes went by before a server cleaned the table. I sat there dumbfounded. The owner never called staff over, nor did he take the opportunity to remind anyone about the need to keep the tables clean. He was more concerned about saving a penny on a coffee cup. He simply didn't care about what customers care about. His vision was all about saving money and not enhancing the customer experience. This lazy practice doesn't have to be the case. A friend of mine works at a Starbucks location, and she says it's their policy to scan the tables every fifteen minutes to make sure they are clear, clean, and ready for the next patron. Starbucks gets it. Apple gets it. But many others do not.

When this restaurant in my town goes out of business—and it will—what do you think the owner will blame? The economy, of course. But it's not about the economy; it's about the experience. Successful business owners care. They care about the people they hire, how they are trained, the quality of the product, the interactions between staff and customers, and the way customers feel when they walk in and when they walk out.

Dirty Toilets and Other Ways to Piss Away Your Customers

The infamous, handwritten "Please let us know if our bathroom needs attention" sign is typically a telltale sign that you are in a much neglected bathroom (and it won't get better after you notify the staff). A friend of mine purposely goes to certain stores and restaurants where he knows the bathrooms are clean and orderly, because he doesn't want to get stuck using a dirty toilet. During an interview for an article I wrote for *Bloomberg Businessweek*, I remember a story Paul Orfalea, founder of Kinko's, now FedEx Office, told me.[10] When he would visit Kinko's locations, one of the first actions he took was to visit the loo, not for the obvious, but to make sure customers were getting the clean, well-stocked bathroom they deserved should the need arise. Not all retail locations have public restrooms available, but the philosophy behind keeping a bathroom clean runs over onto the sales floor.

There are many other ways than offering a dirty bathroom to piss away your customers. In an article for our site, my wife,

Vanessa, posted a list of additional no-no's when it comes to "keeping house:"[11]

- **Bad Breath.** Some people can't help it, literally, but if you are up close and personal to customers regularly, avoid cigarettes, cough drops, peanuts, garlic, onions, and other strong-smelling consumables before your shift.

- **Strong Perfumes and Colognes.** I don't care if your new hot girlfriend just bought you a new spray...lay off. You never know when a customer might get offended.

- **Cobwebs.** Halloween is one night only and revisits once every 365 days. Never should your customers be able to spot spiders and cobwebs.

- **Dust on Objects and Shelves.** This is only acceptable if on the set of *The Phantom of the Opera*.

- **Wrinkles.** Avoid wrinkles in employee attire, table linens, paper menus, programs, or anything else of use to a customer.

- **Stains.** Avoid stains on employee attire, table linens, paper menus, programs, and so on.

- **Holes, Tears, and Damaged Items or Structures.** There are places of business with wobbly tables, rotting holes in the ceiling, and rips in booth seats, just to name a few examples.

- **Pets.** Unless it's a dog shelter or pet shop, business owners and managers should never allow animals into a commercial venue where customers visit. The only exception is guide dogs and other trained animals lawfully assisting their masters. A small dog in a Juicy Couture purse doesn't make the cut either.

This is a short list. I'm sure you have more ideas to add to the list, but you get my point by now: good customer service isn't always determined by what was said to you during your experience, but by how much care, effort, and interest was put into the cleanliness and appeal of the environment your experience took place in. An Apple Store is spotless. There's a reason for it.

A gift card for the Apple Store is pretty much the greatest gift you can give a design nerd. —Paul S.

Be Show Ready

The local restaurant I mentioned earlier is certainly not what Disney calls "show ready." It's nearly impossible to find trash on the ground of a Disney theme park. Everyone is trained to pick up discarded wrappers so the resorts remain clean. If a manager were to walk by trash without picking it up, it would send the wrong message to staff. For a small business that might not have a physical location, this concept can be as simple as making sure your website is clean, professional, and easy to navigate. Your website is your front door. If it's not show ready, it can make or break your business.

At Disney parks, guests are no more than thirty feet from a trash can so there's no excuse to discard anything on the ground. It's believed that Walt Disney was eating an ice cream cone, and when finished, some thirty paces later, he said there needed to be a trash can in that place. Disney has also found that by keeping the grounds spotless, it elevates everyone's behavior, guests included. People are actually embarrassed to be seen littering!

Disneyland, which opened in 1955, was remarkably clean from day one because Walt Disney wanted it that way. When he was developing the concept behind a theme park, Disney visited fairs, circuses, carnivals, and amusement parks around the world. He studied the attractions and the staff. Apparently he didn't like Coney Island because he found the ride operators to be unfriendly. Instead, Disney found his inspiration in Tivoli Gardens in Copenhagen. The employees were warm and courteous, the food was excellent, the music was charming, the colors were bright, and the grounds were meticulously maintained.

There's an old black-and-white photo of Walt Disney himself picking up trash at Disneyland. He cared. So did Steve Jobs. He cared about everything. He once said that everything they do at Apple starts with the question, "How easy will it be for the user?" This question applies to product design and the in-store retail experience. How easy is it to find someone to help you at an Apple Store? Very easy. (You can even purchase accessories yourself with the Apple Retail app without interacting with an employee at all or purchase products online and pick them up in a store. "Personal pickup" became so popular in a short amount of time that employee name tags began promoting the service so that customers would ask more questions about it.) Everything is "easy." That's why Apple employees wear brightly colored shirts with the Apple logo on them. The blue shirt was chosen because the color stood out the best. It's why an iPad is tethered to major products at the Apple Store along with detailed specifications. It's why customers can purchase their items and check out on the floor without standing in a line at a cash register. It's why many Apple Stores are located in shopping malls. Although the real estate was a lot more expensive, Steve Jobs didn't want people to gamble with twenty minutes of their time to visit a computer store in a remote location. He wanted them to gamble with twenty feet of their time. He wanted to make the experience easy.

There are some old adages in retailing—pile it high and let 'em fly, or grab and go. For years retailers simply put products on shelves and tried to get people through the door. Now most large retailers have high-priced consultants who conduct motion studies to track how customers walk around a store and what appeals to their eyes. What they are finding is that most people are attracted to a clean layout, uncluttered displays, clear pricing, and simple signage. In 2001, Steve Jobs and Ron Johnson understood what motion studies and neuroscientists have recently discovered: customers appreciate open space, natural light, unobstructed views, clean stores, and friendly people. If those two men were right about store design well before the rest of the retail world caught up to them, perhaps they were right about the other components of the customer experience as well!

CHECKOUT

1. **Unclutter the retail space.** The last ten years of research have confirmed that open spaces and uncluttered environments make customers feel more relaxed and more receptive to making purchases. Does your store pass the smudge test?

2. **Apply the open space philosophy to your website and marketing material.** Eliminate clutter on your site. Be sparing in the use of content. Study the Apple website (www.apple.com). According to Dr. A. K. Pradeep, the Apple site is the best example of blending content and space to appeal to the buying brain.

3. **Visit and take note.** Visit Apple stores, AT&T retail stores, Tesla Motors, and the new Microsoft stores for design inspiration.

CHAPTER 16

Pay Attention to Design Details

For you to sleep well at night, the aesthetic, the quality, has to be carried all the way through.

—Steve Jobs

An American couple living in the Yunnan Province in China's remote southwest corner walked into what they thought was an Apple Store. It had all the elements: Apple products, an interesting spiral staircase, an upstairs lounge, and staff in blue shirts with name tags. But the American woman noticed something strange about the staircase. It was poorly made, and it showed. The walls had not been painted properly, the staff's name tags had no names, and Apple never writes "Apple Store" on the sign. It just puts up a glowing image of its iconic fruit logo. In the photographs the couple took and published on their blog, wires and cables could clearly be seen cluttering the wooden tabletops instead of hidden from view as they are in real Apple stores. This particular store in Kunming, China, did turn out to be a fake, and other rip-offs were soon discovered, up to twenty-two in total. The fake stores were exposed because Apple pays attention to the details of design and aesthetics. And someone noticed.

Those blue shirts the fake store attempted to copy were the result of paying attention to design details, down to how retail store employees dress. Apple learned that when employees wore black T-shirts, they blended in with their customers. Wearing too many colors resulted in confusion. Blue shirts were just right. Apple makes sure everything is just right, from its shirts to its stores and, of course, its products.

Early Apple investor Mike Markkula defined the principles that would serve as the foundation of the brand. The one-page document, titled "The Apple Marketing Philosophy," stressed three points.[1] First, Apple would have "empathy," understanding the needs of and the feelings of its customers. Second, Apple would focus, eliminating unimportant opportunities. Third, and most important for this chapter, was a concept Markkula called "impute," which meant that people form an opinion about a company based on the impression it creates. A company can have the best, highest quality products, but if those products are presented poorly, it doesn't matter. Markkula was adamant that everything the customer saw—and things the customer didn't see—should create an impression about the brand. The Apple experience begins from the first impression and lasts through every impression moving forward. Apple has passion for the smallest detail. Every design detail matters, and it matters a lot.

Museum of Modern Art Quality

Steve Jobs paid attention to the details, sometimes obsessively so. But nobody would deny that his preciseness made every product better. Jobs paid attention to the details that nobody else saw, and if they did notice, the details would appear to be so inconsequential as to not make a difference. But when those details came together, they did make a difference in the experience customers would have with the brand.

At the elegant, five-level Apple Store in Tokyo's Ginza district, most visitors will tell you that they remember the cool glass elevator that allows them to see each floor. Ask to describe the handrails, and nobody will have noticed. Steve Jobs did. When he visited the Ginza store—a high-profile store because it was the first to open outside the United States—he ordered the stainless steel handrail to be changed because he wanted the mill lines of the steel to wrap around the tube instead of along its length. It was aesthetically more pleasing. Jobs wanted the first Macintosh to have the curves of a Porsche, not a Ferrari. Details mattered. Jobs wanted pop-up dialog boxes on the Mac screen to have rounded corners instead of straight rectangles. Details mattered. Jobs criticized the initial design of the first Mac because the "radius of the first chamfer needs to be bigger, and I don't like the size of the bevel."[2] Details mattered to Jobs.

Two important men shaped Jobs's design aesthetic—his father and the German designer Walter Gropius, who founded the Bauhaus movement. From his dad, Jobs learned the importance of maintaining a commitment to quality and excellence, even when no one else paid attention. "When you're a carpenter making a beautiful chest of drawers, you're not going to use a piece of plywood on the back, even though it faces the wall and nobody will ever see it. You'll know it's there, so you're going to use a beautiful piece of wood on the back,"[3] said Jobs.

Jobs's commitment to design excellence would often drive engineers crazy. When the Macintosh was first being developed in the early 1980s, Jobs disliked the first designs of the printed circuit boards that would hold the chips and other components inside the computer. He thought they were "ugly" because the lines were too close. When engineers countered with the argument that the design did not impact the performance of the PC and that nobody would see the board anyway, Jobs reacted, "I want it to be as beautiful as possible, even if it's inside the box."[4]

In addition to his father's influence, Jobs's design aesthetic was shaped by the Bauhaus movement of industrial design, which stressed simple, elegant, and beautiful design elements. "So that's our approach,"[5] Jobs once proclaimed to his Apple team. "Very simple. We're shooting for Museum of Modern Art quality. The way we're running the company, the product design, the advertising, it all comes down to this: Let's make it simple. Really simple." Here's the problem most brands face when trying to make things simple and elegant—hard work gets in the way. It takes effort, commitment, and courage to keep things simple. Steve Jobs had all three.

Cardboard's Most Demanding Customer

I once visited a manufacturing plant in the central valley town of Modesto, California. I was doing some research for an upcoming speech to a group of manufacturing executives, and some members of the group ran this particular company. The massive building was filled with highly complex equipment to convert corrugated cardboard into all sorts of boxes. Manufacturing product boxes is extremely complex, requiring highly specialized and very expensive equipment to make millions of boxes with displays or ones that are folded in complex dimensions.

This particular manufacturer had many clients, including pharmaceutical companies, food brands, and computer makers. But its most demanding client—far tougher than all the others—was Apple. Every detail matters to Apple: how curves look on the edges of a box, how letters feel to the touch, how easy the boxes are to open. Everything had to enhance the experience customers enjoyed when opening their products. For Apple, corrugated cardboard could be transformed into more than a box. It could be used to create a work of art.

As a result of this obsession with detail in packaging, videos of people "unboxing" Apple products have become unlikely hits on YouTube. If you have a lot of free time on your hands, you can spend countless hours watching thousands of videos of people taking new Macbooks, iPods, iPhones, and iPads out of their boxes. The psychology behind the unboxing phenomenon is simple to understand. In a world of increased clutter, people crave simplicity. When you open an Apple product, the first and only thing you see is the actual device. No cords, manuals, or accessories clutter the first impression. Customers unboxing their products on YouTube seem to enjoy the bold graphics, textures, and the logical way each component is revealed as the layers inside the box are exposed.

Many college students display the boxes proudly in their dorm rooms. It's almost as though people feel that there's something wrong about throwing them away. That's the way Steve Jobs wanted it. He wanted Apple's products, including the packages, to resemble works of art. And art, in Jobs's opinion, could be beautiful on the outside and the inside. "In most people's vocabularies, design means veneer. It's interior decorating. It's the fabric of the curtains, of the sofa. But to me, nothing could be further from the meaning of design. Design is the fundamental soul of a human-made creation that ends up expressing itself in successive outer layers of the product or service,"[6] said Jobs.

> *Apple has an understanding others don't. There's an interface between people and the packages that happens before you even reach the product.* —Laura B.

Moving Mountains Is Worth the Effort

The industrial designer Yves Behar made the argument that Steve Jobs changed everything about the way executives judge the value of design in their products and the retail experience. According to Behar, "Apple's dominance in the smartphone, laptop, digital music, app, and retail integration has stunned (and changed) the world. And Steve's holistic design vision across every aspect of the company is the primary driver for Apple's dominance."[7] Behar says that when people come to his design agency and say, "I want to be the Apple of this or that," he asks them if they are ready to be Steve Jobs. Behar says few people are up to the task. He means that Apple is committed to design excellence in every aspect of the customer experience and that few people have the commitment and courage to do what it takes to stand out. For example, how many of us pay attention to the tile in a store? According to Apple, "We've also learned more than a few things about stone. Like how to reveal granite's true color with a blowtorch. And that sometimes granite has veins of color that have to be matched. We've also learned that getting the details perfect can feel like trying to move a mountain. Sometimes two. But in the end, the effort is worth it. Because steel, glass, and stone can combine to create truly unique and inspiring spaces."[8]

This book is not about retail design. If you want to learn more about glass, wood, or flooring in the Apple Store, there are plenty of resources that track every detail to the exact dimension. The most comprehensive is Gary Allen's blog, ifoapplestore.com. Read Gary's blog to learn things such as:

- Tables are made of Canadian sugar maple, and they are enormously complex to make and assemble.

- Ceilings in many stores are made of specialized, one-piece plastic material stretched over perimeter frames.

- Tiles are thirty-inch squares of Pietra Serena sandstone mined from the Sienna district of Italy (outside of Florence).

Design details should matter to everyone, regardless of what field they are in. Design matters. Is your website easy to navigate? Good design will make it easy for your customers to find what they want. Is your content easy to understand? Is your product simple and intuitive? Design counts and details matter in all areas of your business, but especially in the area of customer service. Let's look at how two companies, one large and one small, pay attention to design details to create unique experiences in one of the most commoditized categories—coffee.

Rekindling the Romance at Starbucks

On January 8, 2008, Howard Schultz reclaimed his title as CEO of Starbucks after an eight-year hiatus. The brand had lost its way. Sales were in a free fall, the stock price was plunging, fewer people were going to Starbucks, and those who did visit were spending less. The company had to eliminate 12,000 positions and close 600 stores. Over the next three years, Starbucks would regain its mojo, recording its highest sales ever and seeing its stock price hit all-time highs despite an ongoing global recession.

Schultz's return to Starbucks started nearly a year earlier on February 14, 2007, when a stinging memo he wrote to internal leadership was unwittingly made public. In the memo, Schultz had expressed his displeasure with what he called the commoditization of the Starbucks experience. When I read the memo, Schultz's attention to details stood out for me. Read through the following points that Schultz made in his e-mail, and ask yourself whether you would have considered these details to describe the decline in the Starbucks experience that Schultz observed. According to Schultz, here is where Starbucks had lost its way.

- When we went to automatic espresso machines, we solved a major problem in terms of speed of service and efficiency. At the same time we overlooked the fact that we would remove much of the romance and theater that was in play.[9]

- The height of the new machines blocked the visual sight line the customer previously had to watch the drink being made and for the intimate experience with the barista.

- The need for fresh-roasted coffee moved us toward the decision and the need for flavor locked packaging…we achieved fresh-roasted, bagged coffee, but at what cost? The loss of aroma—perhaps the most powerful nonverbal signal we had in our stores; the loss of our people scooping fresh coffee from the bins and grinding it fresh in front of the customer.

- Stores no longer have the soul of the past and reflect a chain of stores versus the warm feeling of a neighborhood store. Some people even call our stores sterile, cookie cutter, no longer reflecting the passion our partners feel about our coffee.

When Schultz returned as the Starbucks CEO, one of his strategic initiatives was to reignite the emotional attachment with customers. "The equity of the Starbucks brands was steeped in the unique experience customers have from the moment they walk into the store,"[10] said Schultz. He believed that stores can make emotional connections through the stories they tell. And everything tells the story. "Ideally, every Starbucks store should tell a story about coffee and what we as an organization believe in. That story should unfold via the taste and presentation of our products as well as the sights, sounds, and smells that surround our customers. The aroma of freshly ground coffee. Interior hues, textures, the shapes and materials of furniture and fixtures as well as their origins. The art on the walls. The music. The rhythm of the coffee bar and how our partners move and speak behind the counter—and what they speak about." Schultz went as far as closing every Starbucks for several hours to retrain every barista and to recapture the art of making coffee.

According to Schultz, the baristas—the customer facing employees who are largely responsible for creating the Starbucks experience—had lost their passion because they were not learning the Starbucks story or being reminded of its mission. They were being handed three-ring binders with rules, techniques, and information, and they were told to read it. For too many employees—Starbucks calls them "partners"—Starbucks had become a job. And as you know by now, once your employees think of their roles as nothing but a job, the passion and commitment to excellence will start to wane.

After Schultz's return to Starbucks, one of the first people he called for advice was Steve Jobs. Both leaders returned to the helm of the companies they started when the future looked bleak. They both succeeded in revitalizing their brands and transforming entire product categories. Jobs reminded Schultz to get the details of the experience just right. By doing so, Schultz was able to reinvigorate the experience and return Starbucks to his original vision of a third place between work and home, an oasis where people could feel uplifted, comforted, and connected.

Turning a Commodity into an Experience

Walk into Funnel Mill Rare Coffee & Tea on Broadway near Ninth Street in Santa Monica, California, and you'll feel like you entered a traditional tea garden. Soft music, a beautiful waterfall, and the aroma of freshly roasted beans are just the beginning of the experience. Funnel Mill's owner, J. C. Ho, has banned the use of cell phones as well as the snapping of photographs. He did so after some of his customers, film directors and movie stars, made the requests. These are just some of the many ways J. C. has transformed coffee from a commodity product into a remarkable experience that has turned his restaurant into a popular coffee lounge for the rich and famous Hollywood set.

First, the Funnel Mill experience begins with a vision to offer an exceptional level of customer service. Ho told me that when he was working for a computer company, he traveled around the world and enjoyed dropping into coffee shops. But something was always missing. He never discovered a perfect combination of quality and service. "The coffee shops would either offer good food and horrible service or good service and horrible food,"[11] he told me.

J. C. and his wife, Teresa, knew they wanted to start a business, and the coffee experience—or lack of one in many places—offered an opportunity to succeed on their own. Most people would have thought the couple was crazy for entering a market crowded with national chains with far more name recognition than they could hope to achieve. But Ho was undeterred because he realized that a superior customer experience could spell success in any field.

J. C. and Teresa spent five years researching the industry and developing a business plan before they opened their store. On their first day they worked from 4:00 a.m. to 10:00 p.m. and made $17. Despite the slow start, word began to spread, and soon people began to learn that Funnel Mill offered more than coffee and tea; it made exceptionally high-quality coffee and tea drinks with a shot of friendliness. It also paid attention to details most stores and restaurants would easily overlook. Funnel Mill carefully considers every detail.

- **Open Space.** J.C. wants to make customers feel relaxed when they enter his lounge, if only for a few minutes during their otherwise hectic day. Fountains evoke a traditional, soothing tea garden. The furniture, made of imported Taiwanese wood, is arranged so customers don't bump into each other or jostle for a place to sit. At Apple, glass is used to make the retail space lighter and display tables made of wood give warmth to the space. Accessories are placed on side walls so as not to distract customers from the featured attractions—the products on the display tables. Just as Apple does for computers, J.C. understands the roles of space, glass, and wood to create an inviting atmosphere.

- **Greetings.** In most cases, Funnel Mill customers are greeted with a smile and a warm, friendly "hello" before they reach the counter. Sound familiar?

- **Open Display Area.** J.C. doesn't have computers to display, but he still provides theater. The area where J.C. and his staff prepare drinks is open and easy to see because he uses a unique and visual process to make coffee, called "siphoning." The technique was invented in the 1830s and is very visual. Customers can see J.C. mix, measure, and boil the ideal combination of espresso, water, and milk to create the best coffee I've ever had. It's visual because the equipment resembles something you'd find in a chemistry lab. The process results in an incredibly rich cup of coffee. Most coffee shops don't use this process, because it requires specialized training, expensive equipment, and time. It takes three to four minutes for an experienced person to prepare each cup.

- **Power Outlets.** They are everywhere to accommodate customers who want to use their computers.

- **Furniture.** J.C. imports unique, elegant wooden tables or provides comfortable leather couches arranged to facilitate conversations and informal meetings.

- **Commitment to Quality.** J.C. purchases only the highest grades of tea and coffee beans that meet his exacting standards.

- **Unique Items.** J.C. offers unique items not found in the coffee chain one block away, such as the rare Kopi Luwak coffee. At $65 a cup, it's all the rage with the Hollywood elite. What's so special about it? Well, it tastes very, very good. It's quite likely the best coffee you've ever had. But its origin might turn you off. It comes from the island of Sumatra where a small mammal called a palm civet eats coffee cherries, including the bean inside. Once the bean finishes its journey through the animal's digestive tract, the intact beans are harvested, cleaned, and roasted. Yes, it's literally made from animal poop. I'm not sure how many customers actually order the coffee, but people in town talk about it and they know Funnel Mill offers it. It's a hook that helps word of mouth.

- **Water Filtration System.** Many restaurants use tap water, and some will use a basic filter. But that's not good enough for a coffee lounge that wants to raise the bar on the customer experience. Coffee is 98 percent water, and that convinced J.C. to purchase the best water filtration system on the market. It softens the water, uses reverse osmosis to remove contaminants, and even pumps minerals back into the water after the particles have been removed. Details matter.

- **Consistent Delivery.** I visit Funnel Mill once every two months on business trips to Santa Monica, and each time I go the "packaging" of the product is consistent. Again, no detail is overlooked. Here is how J.C. explained it:

> Coffees are brought on silver platters. At the twelve o'clock position, we place two types of sugars in small ceramic bowls so you can see how clean and pure the sugar is. The drink is placed at the six o'clock position with the handle positioned at the four o'clock position to make it easy for the customer to pick it up while they're working on their computer. A napkin and a long-stem spoon is placed in the nine o'clock position, and the customer's choice of cream is placed at three o'clock. Our ingredients are measured to the gram. I want to make sure that your drink tastes and looks the same each and every time. The experience must be consistent whether you come in tomorrow or a year from now.[12]

J.C. is obsessed with detail. Schultz is obsessed with detail, and so was Steve Jobs.

In a sad but very revealing story in the Walter Isaacson biography, we learn that Jobs pushed away an oxygen mask during one of his operations for a liver transplant. He demanded to see other options because he didn't like the design of the mask. Jobs's curse became our blessing. Jobs brought beauty to technology and reminded us that retail spaces could be more than four walls used to store and distribute products. They could be architectural landmarks. Apple's New York City Fifth Avenue "cube" is one of the most photographed sites in the entire city. Ironically, the past history of the location had failed for other retailers because the site is underground. But where most people saw an underground failure, Jobs and his designer, Peter Bohlin, saw a "ceremony of descent."

Apple continues to demand precision and excellence in everything it does, choosing to focus on every detail of design and the customer experience. They say the devil's in the details. For Apple the details make the experience positively heavenly.

CHECKOUT

1. **Review every detail of your customer experience, including every aspect of design.** Consider it from your customer's view: website, packaging, physical design. Are all the design elements of your "location" (physical and virtual) telling the brand story that you want to convey?

2. **Develop a consistent experience.** Train yourself and your staff to make every experience memorable for each and every customer and from one day to the next by minding the details and not slacking off.

3. **Strive for what Jobs called "Museum of Modern Art quality."** What people don't see is often what matters the most if only because it forces you to pay attention to design throughout the entire customer experience.

CHAPTER 17

Design Multisensory Experiences

*Our stores are designed to create
owners of Apple products and
build loyalty.*

—Apple mantra

The screens on MacBook computers are set at ninety-degree angles in an Apple Store. The screen's position forces you to touch the computer, moving the screen to your ideal viewing angle. In One to One workshops, Creatives don't touch the computer without permission. Instead they guide customers to find the solutions themselves. Everything is connected in the Apple Store for the purpose of encouraging customers to touch, play, and interact with the devices. iPads are connected to the Internet. iMacs, iPod Touches, and MacBooks are as well. Although the products have changed since the first Apple Store opened, connectivity is still a key component of the experience.

When Steve Jobs gave a tour of the first Apple Store in 2001, he highlighted the fact that all of the computers were connected to the Internet. "You can go up to any computer and start surfing, go to your personal website, or do whatever

Woman touching iPad in an Apple Store. *Source:* Getty Images

you want to do on the Internet. It's pretty great,"[1] he said. You can still walk up to any device in the store and start using it—read books on an iPad, play games on an iPod Touch, listen to music on an iPod, or create a presentation on a MacBook, or view photos on an iMac. Steve Jobs intuitively understood that there's power in touch. By giving Apple's customers the ability to manipulate the devices for themselves and to play, learn, and have fun, customers would be able to immerse themselves in the ownership experience.

Ron Johnson and Steve Jobs reimagined the retail experience by creating a store that's more than a store to people. At Apple this meant giving customers the ability to try before they buy, to bring the joy back to the shopping, and to make the store fun. It meant giving more than lip service to "customer engagement." It meant that the ownership experience was more important than the sale. According to an Apple marketing document designed to celebrate the Apple Store's tenth anniversary, "around the time we opened the store in Tysons Corner, in 2001, everyone else was trying to talk to their customers less. Which made us think that maybe we should talk to them more. Face-to-face if possible."[2] Apple knew that its stores can and should be centers for creativity. Multisensory experiences were the heart of it.

A few days prior to the first store opening in 2001, Apple placed an ad in national newspapers. The headline read, "5 down. 95 to go." The text of the ad explains the headline and explains how Apple intended to reimagine the retail experience.

> Apple currently has 5 percent market share in personal computers. This means that out of one hundred computer users, five of them use Macs. While that may not sound like a lot, it is actually higher than both BMW's and Mercedes-Benz's share of the automotive market. And it equals 25 million customers around the world using Macs. But that's not enough for us. We want to convince the other 95 people that Macintosh offers a much simpler, richer, and human-centric computing experience. And we believe the best way to do this is to open stores right in their neighborhoods. Stores that let people experience firsthand what it's like to make a movie on a Mac. Or burn a CD with their favorite music. Or take pictures with a digital camera and publish them on their personal website. Or select from over 300 software titles, including some of the best educational titles for kids. Or talk to a Macintosh Genius at our Genius Bar. Because if only 5 of those remaining 95 people switch to Macs, we'll double our market share and, more importantly, earn the chance to delight another 25 million customers. Here we go...[3]

Apple did succeed in doubling its market share and in the process built a store that inspires retailers to elevate the customer experience. "He [Jobs] didn't ask, 'How do we build a phone that can achieve a 2 percent market share?' He asked, 'How do we reinvent the telephone?'"[4] said Ron Johnson. "In the same way, retailers shouldn't be asking, 'How do we create a store that's going to do $15 million a year?' They should be asking, 'How do we reinvent the store to enrich our customers' lives?'"

Building a Friend for Life

Apple is perfecting the notion of experience shopping for computers while Build-A-Bear has done so for teddy bears. By allowing children to participate in the actual creation of their stuffed animals, the store has moved beyond a toy store to one that creates treasured childhood memories. Two years after their first Build-A-Bear experience, my daughters remember choosing their animals and the outfits they would wear. They also remember making a wish and watching as the animals' "heart" was stuffed into the casing. Build-A-Bear learned long ago that kids love to create and that families enjoy interactive experiences together. In fact Build-A-Bear is not called a "store," but a "workshop." Its mission is to bring the teddy bear to life and to evoke warm thoughts about childhood. Anyone can sell a stuffed animal, but Build-A-Bear won the hearts and minds of millions of children around the world by turning the commodity into a multisensory experience.

> *Time and again Apple shows what good customer service really means.* —John P.

Rock the Aisle

Dr. A. K. Pradeep says the brain loves multisensory experiences. The more you engage the senses, the more likely it is that the brain engages with the product or service on an emotional level. This stimulates information retention and, not surprisingly, the willingness to buy. By encouraging customers to touch and play with products, Apple and LEGO stores are satisfying a core subconscious need. According to Pradeep, "Superior shopping experiences are those that enable consumers to walk away not only having absorbed a lot of information, but having extracted insight that becomes part of an educational experience. Education is more than information. It is distilled insights that can be used on an ongoing basis."[5]

Pradeep also believes entertainment plays a key role, in addition to information and education. "A huge benefit of modern life is the luxury of being entertained while we shop. This is such a compelling feature of the experience that we seek it out whenever we can. The combination of shopping (which the brain more or less equates with hunting and gathering) and entertainment is enormously powerful."[6]

The Apple Store is fun. It's entertaining. And that's the way Steve Jobs wanted it. At any given time you can see Creatives teaching a customer to edit a video, a group of seniors learning to use an iPad, parents and their children learning to make songs together in a youth workshop, teachers taking kids on field trips to learn and create things, children playing games on an iMac in the "family room" section of the store, while others are attending an event in the Apple theater. Apple likes to say that people come to shop but they return to learn. Apple has turned the boring sales floor into a playground for kids and adults. Jobs and Johnson didn't just "reimagine" the retail experience, they blew it up and started over. According to Johnson, "The retailers that win the future are the ones that start from scratch and figure out how to create fundamentally new types of value for customers."[7]

> *Just booked my first Apple One to One session for tomorrow so I can become a Keynote Jedi.* —Dean W.

Reinventing the Car-Buying Experience the Apple Way

Former Apple Store executives like Tesla vice president George Blankenship are well aware of the power of multisensory emotional experiences. In developing Tesla's concept stores, Blankenship didn't just apply some of the Apple Store principles to the car-buying experience, he copied them exactly. The only difference is that Tesla sells cars and Apple sells computers. Among the similarities:

- **Upscale Location.** Tesla stores are located in upscale shopping malls in places like Fashion Island in Newport Beach and Santana Row, San Jose, or the Oakbrook Center in Illinois. Just as Steve Jobs didn't think that people would gamble with twenty minutes of their time to try out new Apple computers in 2001, Tesla's cars are so different that the store would rather be seen in places where people are spending their time anyway.

- **Open Space.** Tesla dealerships are sparkling clean, uncluttered, brightly lit, and white.

- **Interactive Displays.** Large interactive digital displays invite people to create their own cars, choosing colors, interiors, and other accessories. Then with a swipe of their finger, they can "throw" it to a wall-size display on the back wall where an image of the car they built fills the entire screen. Multisensory, hands-on displays and exhibits give the casual shopper a feeling of what it's like to own a Tesla.

- **Friendly Associates.** They do not work on commission. They are trained not to "sell cars" but instead to make sure that everyone walks out the door with a smile. The goal is to inform, engage, and excite people who enter the store. Tesla hires people who are enthusiastic about the technology and its opportunity to change the world. When people learn something new in a low-pressure, relaxed setting, they are more likely to feel better—and different—than in any other retail experience they've had in the past.

Just as Apple is not in the business of selling cars, Tesla is not in the business of selling computers. It's in the business of teaching people something new, making them feel good, and putting smiles on their faces. Now that's reinventing the car-buying experience!

An internal discussion took place early in the history of the Apple Retail Store. The original vision was to make Apple the best place to *buy* a computer. Jobs and his retail team realized that it was the wrong approach. Apple, they decided, should be the best place to *own* a computer. The ability to interact with devices, to learn, to get help, to get started, and to acquire knowledge about products and software all enhance the ownership experience.

Disney Dreams Bigger

An executive who had the task of reinventing the Disney Store turned to Disney's largest shareholder, Steve Jobs, for advice. Jobs offered these two words: dream bigger. No better advice has even been given. "Steve provided us with inspiration and support. He encouraged us to think big,"[8] said James Fielding, president of Disney Stores Worldwide.

Fielding says the old stores lacked excitement for a company that represents creativity and wonder. It was a serious problem. Fielding says the new stores "should not just be another place to buy Disney stuff but rather a physical manifestation of what Disney creates." By 2016, all of Disney's stores will reflect the new concept model. People can buy Disney products at many retailers, so the Disney Store will become an interactive playground to celebrate the brand. A little girl waving a magic wand in the princess neighborhood can call up Belle from *Beauty and the Beast* or Jasmine from *Aladdin* who suddenly appear. An image of Buzz Lightyear from *Toy Story* might suddenly begin to fly around the store. Meanwhile Disney movies might be shown in the theater, while character-drawing workshops are taking place in another area of the store. "Apple stores revolutionized retail," said Fielding. "But it's not like we were the new kids on the block. We wanted to get back to our heritage."

Disney looks to Apple to regain its "heritage" in creating excitement for its retail store guests. Shouldn't the rest of us? Ron Johnson once said that there's no one formula that works for every business or every retailer. Every business must find the unique formula that works best for it. But he does recommend that businesses start from scratch to create a formula that will help them win the future. There is one big lesson that we can all take away from Apple's success. Stop trying to figure out how to sell something to somebody; figure out how you want your customers to *feel*. That's the Apple way.

CHECKOUT

1. **Start from scratch.** Try this exercise to kick-start some creative ideas. Ask yourself, "How do we want our customers to feel when they experience our brand?" The answer will be much different than asking the standard question, "How are we going to grow our sales by *x* percent next year?" Starting from scratch means asking new questions.

2. **Create multisensory experiences for your clients or customers.** Even if you do not own a retail establishment, you can create such moments by adding video and stories to your website or reimagining how you deliver presentations. Masterful communicators

go beyond the slides to inspire their audiences through auditory, visual, and kinesthetic means. One of my earlier books, *The Presentation Secrets of Steve Jobs*, has transformed the way hundreds of thousands of individuals and businesses around the word create, craft, and deliver presentations. Multisensory experiences are at the heart of breathtaking presentations.

3. **Bombard the brain with new experiences.** Visit a Lush store to see how the staff creates multisensory events where customers can physically experience its soap and bath products in-store. Plan a trip to Las Vegas and visit one of the newest hotels, The Cosmopolitan. The hotel has created one of the most unique experiences on "The Strip" with images, lights, and space unlike anything you've ever seen in a hotel. You don't have $3 billion to replicate the experience back home, but you'll be inspired to think differently about the experience you do provide. Steve Jobs once said, "Creativity is connecting things." He meant that creativity comes from seeking out new experiences. It's why Jobs studied calligraphy in college. If he hadn't, the Macintosh might not have been the first computer with beautiful font and typography, pioneering the desktop publishing revolution. It's why he visited an ashram in India. It's why he carefully looked at kitchen appliances at Macy's before building the Apple II. It's why he studied the Four Seasons, The Ritz-Carlton, and other customer service champions before opening the Apple Store. Jobs believed that a broad set of experiences helped him develop creative, groundbreaking ideas.

The Soul of Apple

Just make it great.

—Steve Jobs

The Apple Retail Store does not sell products. It enriches lives and, by doing so, has become the most profitable retailer on the planet. Apple's customer service scores are the envy of the industry because its employees (Specialists, Creatives, Experts, and Geniuses) strive to make customer experiences memorable and magical. Jobs once told former Apple CEO John Sculley that it's better to be a pirate than to join the navy. In other words, break away from convention and what's ordinary. The ordinary is to sell products. The vision behind the Apple Store is to enrich lives. That's extraordinary.

While I was researching this book, people close to me would ask, "Who are you writing this book for? Retailers?" The answer soon became obvious. This book is for anyone who has a business that deals with people. Sure, it includes retailers in any category. But it also includes small business owners, entrepreneurs, managers, CEOs, lawyers, accountants, doctors, sales professionals, department supervisors, and anyone who sells a service or a product. It's for anyone who is serious about reimagining the customer experience, because at its core, this book is not about Apple. It's about the *soul* of Apple—its people.

Most people don't know why they feel good in an Apple Store, they just do. But it's people who elevate the customer experience— people who are inspired, are passionate, and have been given the resources and taught the communication techniques required to turn transactions into experiences. Apple values dynamic and interesting people who are passionate about the brand. Apple offers stimulating work environments designed to enhance careers and develop lifelong skills. Apple values innovation, embraces change, and seeks feedback from its employees and customers. Apple celebrates diversity and gives employees and customers the opportunity to reach their highest form of self-expression. Apple creates a community dedicated to open communication and commitment to its customers every day. Apple inspires and creates a happy place for people to work and for customers to learn. Inspire people and anything can happen.

It Makes Our Hearts Sing

Seven months before he passed away, Steve Jobs took to the stage to introduce the iPad 2. He was noticeably thin and weaker than usual. But his deteriorating health didn't stop him from putting a smile on his face and briefly telling the audience what he believed about creating products and experiences. Jobs's words are worth remembering:

> It's in Apple's DNA that technology alone is not enough. It's technology married with liberal arts, married with the humanities, that yields us the results that makes our hearts sing. And nowhere is that more true than in these post-PC devices. A lot of folks in this tablet market are rushing in and they're looking at this as the next PC. They're talking about speeds and feeds just like they did with PCs. Our experience and every bone in our body says that that is not the right approach. These post-PC devices need to be even easier to use than a PC. Even more intuitive than a PC. We think we're on the right track with this. We

think we have the right architecture not just in silicon, but in the organization to build these kinds of products.[1]

The products Jobs envisioned continue to delight young and old the world over, but it's the *experience* those customers have with those products that make them return again and again.

I mentioned earlier that my daughter Josephine was six years old when I took her to the Apple Store for the first time. She had never touched an iPad before but started navigating it like a pro in a matter of seconds. Josephine turned to me, smiled, and said, "I *love* this store!" Now you know why. If you can delight your customers and make them feel joyful, you know you're on to something.

Steve Jobs was passionate about building a company that lasts. He told biographer Walter Isaacson that his most important professional goal was to do what his heroes Bill Hewlett and David Packard had done, which was to build a company so imbued with innovation and creativity that it would outlive them. Life is far too short to give anything you do a half-baked effort. Steve encouraged us to live a life of excellence, and that excellence extends to how you treat your employees and how they, in turn, treat the customer. Give your customers an experience to remember, and they'll help you build a legacy to be proud of.

Average Is Over

"Average is officially over,"[2] declares Thomas Friedman in his book *That Used to Be Us.* "What was 'average' work ten years ago is below average today and will be further below average ten years from now... As a result everyone needs to raise his or her game just to stay in place, let alone get ahead of other workers. What was an average performance in the past will not earn an average grade, an average wage, or a middle class standard of living." Friedman believes that everyone should be asking if what they are doing is unique and irreplaceable. "Am I putting some extra chocolate, whipped cream, and a cherry on top of whatever I do?" he suggests asking.

In the hyperconnected world that Friedman describes, anyone who wants to start a business has more resources available than ever before, far more than Steve Jobs and Steve Wozniak had in 1976 when they started Apple in the garage of Jobs's parents' house in Los Altos, California. But unless that entrepreneur offers something "extra" or above average, it doesn't matter.

Even those who are not entrepreneurs must reinvent themselves within their companies if they hope to remain relevant in an increasingly complex and competitive global environment. "For many others it will mean becoming a creative server and bringing a special passion or human touch to a job in a way that truly enriches the experience for the person paying for it,"[3] says Friedman.

> You see it when you are waited on by a salesperson in the men's suit department or the women's shoe department who is so engaging, so up on the latest fashions and able to make you look your best that you'll come back and ask for that person by name. You see it in that trainer or Pilates instructor who seems to know exactly how to teach each exercise properly— the one everyone is standing in line for, even though he charges more than his colleagues. And you see it on Southwest Airlines, where they manage to take an economy seat and give it something extra.

And you see it in the Apple Store and in every retailer in the past ten years that Apple has inspired to raise its game.

Just Make It Great

During an interview on *Charlie Rose*, Pixar chief John Lasseter told a short, insightful story about Steve Jobs. Steve had purchased Pixar for $10 million from George Lucas in 1986. Jobs lost money on Pixar every quarter for nine straight years, pumping $50 million of his own money into the company. But he believed in the people and their vision to create digitally animated movies that would enrich the lives of moviegoers of any age.

When Jobs was thinking of returning to Apple in 1997, he sought Lasseter's permission. He didn't need to, of course, but Pixar held a special place in Jobs's heart. He told Lasseter, "The reason why I'm going back is because I think the world is a better place with Apple in it, and they're not going to survive."⁴ Jobs believed the world was a better place with Pixar in it, as well. Jobs told Lasseter, "The way people feel about our brand [Pixar] is the way people felt about Apple. It's like a bank account. We have the opportunity to put deposits in the bank account by making a great product, something they really love, or we can do withdrawals, putting something out there that we know is not good enough but still putting our name on to it."

To Steve Jobs every single thing Pixar did had to be great. He wanted Pixar to always aim high. In Lasseter's first meeting with Jobs, when Lasseter was just one of four animators in the company that Jobs had purchased from Lucas, Lasseter wanted to tell Jobs about a short film he was working on. Jobs's only piece of advice: just make it great. That short, *Tin Toy*, became Pixar's first animated film to win an Academy Award.

Just make it great. If you are fortunate enough to make a product, offer a service, or back a cause that brings value to people's lives, then you owe it to them and to yourself to make it great. By doing so, you move society forward. Avoid the mistake of just focusing on the product or service. Instead, create a magical customer experience that enriches people's lives. Just make it great—insanely great!

Notes

Introduction: Enriching Lives

1. YouTube, "Mark Malkoff: Apple Store Challenge," YouTube, http://www
   .youtube.com/watch?v=Bo2p82aTQzo (accessed December 31, 2011).
2. Ron Johnson, "What I Learned Building the Apple Store," *Harvard Business
   Review*, November, 21, 2011, http://blogs.hbr.org/cs/2011/11/what_i_
   learned_building_the_ap.html (accessed December 31, 2011).
3. Ibid.

PART I: INSPIRING YOUR INTERNAL CUSTOMER

1. Nikki Blacksmith and Jim Harter, "Majority of American Workers Not
   Engaged in Their Jobs," Gallup, October 28, 2011, http://www.gallup.com/
   poll/150383/Majority-AmericanWorkers-Not-Engaged-Jobs.aspx (accessed
   December 31, 2011).

Chapter 1: Dream Bigger

1. Isadore Sharp, *Four Seasons: The Story of a Business Philosophy* (NY: Penguin
   Group, 2009), xv.
2. Ibid., 95.
3. Michael Basch, *Customer Culture: How FedEx and Other Great Companies
   Put the Customer First Every Day* (Upper Saddle River, NJ: FT Prentice
   Hall, 2003), 12.
4. Ibid., 9.
5. Ibid., 24.

6. Ron Johnson, ThinkEquity Conference 2006, posted on www
   .ifoAppleStore.com, http://www.ifoapplestore.com/stores/thinkequity_
   2006_rj.html (accessed December 31, 2011).

Chapter 2: Hire for Smiles

1. Steve Lohr, "The Power of Taking the Big Chance," *The New York Times,*
   October 8, 2011, http://www.nytimes.com/2011/10/09/business/steve-jobs-
   and-the-power-of-taking-the-big-chance.html?pagewanted=all (accessed
   December 31, 2011).
2. Apple website. Jobs at Apple, http://www.apple.com/jobs/us/welcome.html
   (accessed November 6, 2011).
3. ifoAppleStore.com, "10th Apple Poster," http://www.ifoapplestore.com/db/
   10th-anniversary-poster/ (accessed December 31, 2011).
4. CareerBuilder.com, "Personality Trumps Intelligence in Hiring, Study
   Says," CareerBuilder.com, June 9, 2011, http://www.careerbuilder.com/
   Article/CB-2544-Hospitality-Personality-trumps-intelligence-in-hiring-
   study-says/ (accessed December 31, 2011).
5. Bill Taylor, "Hire for Attitude, Train for Skill," *Harvard Business Review,*
   February 1, 2011, http://blogs.hbr.org/taylor/2011/02/hire_for_attitude_
   train_for_sk.html (accessed December 31, 2011).
6. Ibid.
7. Adam Bryant, "Job Interviews Lead with 2 Big Questions," *The New York
   Times,* August 27, 2011, http://www.nytimes.com/2011/08/28/business/
   a-boss-who-believes-nice-isnt-a-bad-word.html?pagewanted=all (accessed
   December 31, 2011).
8. Ibid.
9. You're the Boss, "Can an Applebee's Franchisee Be a Real Entrepreneur?"
   The New York Times, September 14, 2011, http://boss.blogs.nytimes.com/
   tag/zane-tankel/ (accessed December 31, 2011).
10. *Triumph of the Nerds,* PBS documentary DVD, directed by Paul Sen (1996;
    New York: Ambrose Video, 2002).
11. Walter Isaacson, *Steve Jobs* (NY: Simon & Schuster, 2011), 114.

Chapter 3: Cultivate Fearless Employees

1. Walter Isaacson, *Steve Jobs* (NY: Simon & Schuster, 2011), 564.
2. Ibid., 460.
3. YouTube, "Steve Jobs and NeXT," YouTube, http://www.youtube.com/
   watch?v=sOlqqriBvUM (accessed December 31, 2011).
4. Gary Allen, blogger, www.ifoAppleStore.com, in discussion with the author,
   October 11, 2011.
5. Ibid.
6. Walter Isaacson, *Steve Jobs* (NY: Simon & Schuster, 2011), 460.
7. Ibid., 122.
8. Terry Francona, *"On Leadership,"* Opinions, *The Washington Post,* July 21,
   2009, http://www.washingtonpost.com/wp-dyn/content/video/
   2009/07/21/VI2009072102824.html (accessed December 31, 2011).

9. Men's Wearhouse, "Creating Fearless and Energized Workplaces," Men's Wearhouse, http://www.menswearhouse.com/webapp/wcs/stores/servlet/ ContentAttachmentView_-1_10601_10051_10652_10708_10684_ CreatingFearlessWorkplace.html_ (accessed December 31, 2011).
10. Working Life, "Do Us a Favor, Take a Vacation," *Bloomberg Businessweek*, May 21, 2007, http://www.businessweek.com/magazine/content/07_21/ b4035088.htm (accessed December 31, 2011).
11. YouTube, "Steve Jobs Narrates Apple's 'The Crazy Ones' TV ad," http:// www.youtube.com/watch?v=NJzzu7ueZ7U&feature=related (accessed December 31, 2011).
12. uApple, "A Celebration of Steve's Life," Apple, October 19, 2011, http:// events.apple.com.edgesuite.net/10oiuhfvojb23/event/index.html (accessed December 31, 2011).

Chapter 4: Build Trust

1. Stephen M. R. Covey with Rebecca R. Merrill, *The Speed of Trust: The One Thing That Changes Everything* (NY: Free Press, 2006), 21.
2. Ibid., xxv.
3. Apple Store credo card, anonymously given to author.
4. Covey, op.cit., p. 229.
5. Michael Lombardo and Robert Eichinger, *FYI/For Your Improvement: A Guide for Development and Coaching; For Learners, Managers, Mentors, and Feedback Givers*, 5th edition (Minneapolis, MN: Lominger International, 2009), 180.
6. Covey, op.cit., p. 146.

Chapter 5: Foster a Feedback Loop

1. John Baldoni, "Hire People Who Disagree with You," *Harvard Business Review*, July 27, 2009, http://events.apple.com.edgesuite.net/10oiuhfvojb23/ event/index.html (accessed December 31, 2011).
2. Apple Store credo card, anonymously given to author.
3. Nikki Blacksmith and Jim Harter, "Majority of American Workers Not Engaged in Their Jobs," Gallup, October 28, 2011, http://www.gallup.com/ poll/150383/Majority-AmericanWorkers-Not-Engaged-Jobs.aspx (accessed December 31, 2011).
4. Fred Reichheld with Rob Markey, *The Ultimate Question 2.0: How Net Promoter Companies Thrive in a Customer-Driven World* (Boston, MA: Harvard Business School Publishing, 2011), 4.
5. Ibid., 28.
6. Ibid., 2.
7. Ibid., 132.
8. Ibid., 133.
9. Apple customer feedback survey e-mailed to author on November 1, 2011.
10. David Lazarus, "US Airways Could Add Some Humanity to Its 'Corporate Personhood,'" *Los Angeles Times*, October 25, 2011, http://articles.latimes.com/ 2011/oct/25/business/la-fi-lazarus-20111025 (accessed December 31, 2011).

11. Reichheld op.cit., p. 284.
12. Walter Isaacson, *Steve Jobs* (NY: Simon & Schuster, 2011), 569.

Chapter 6: Develop Multitaskers

1. Carolyn DiPiero, Apple customer, in discussion with the author, November 3, 2011.
2. Colin Shaw, Qaalfa Dibeehi, and Steven Walden, *Customer Experience: Future Trends & Insights* (NY: Palgrave Macmillan, 2010), 122.
3. Vanessa Gallo, business manager of Gallo Communications Group, in discussion with the author, October 1, 2011.
4. http://www.todaysworkplace.org/2010/07/06/extreme_customer_service/

Chapter 7: Empower Your Employees

1. ifoAppleStore.com, "10th Apple Poster," http://www.ifoapplestore.com/db/10th-anniversary-poster/ (accessed December 31, 2011).
2. Nikki Blacksmith and Jim Harter, "Majority of American Workers Not Engaged in Their Jobs," Gallup, October 28, 2011, http://www.gallup.com/poll/150383/Majority-AmericanWorkers-Not-Engaged-Jobs.aspx (accessed December 31, 2011).
3. The Ritz-Carlton, "Service Values: I Am Proud to Be Ritz-Carlton," The Ritz-Carlton website, About Us, Gold Standards, http://corporate.ritzcarlton.com/en/about/goldstandards.htm (accessed December 31, 2011).
4. Carmine Gallo, *Fire Them Up!: 7 Simple Secrets to Inspire Colleagues, Customers, and Clients; Sell Yourself, Your Vision, and Your Values; and Communicate with Charisma and Confidence* (NY: John Wiley & Sons, Inc., 2007), 103–104.
5. Daniel Pink, *Drive: The Surprising Truth About What Motivates Us* (NY, Riverhead Books, 2009), 9.
6. Ibid., 35.
7. Ibid., 134.
8. Jack Welch, *Straight from the Gut, Jack Welch* (NY: Warner Business Books, 2001), 29.
9. Gallo, op.cit., p. 151.
10. Ibid.,152.
11. Ibid., 153.
12. Stanford University, "'You've Got to Find What You Love,' Jobs Says," *Stanford Report*, June 14, 2005, Steve Jobs Commencement Address, delivered on June 12, 2005, http://news-service.stanford.edu/news/2005/june15/jobs-061505.html (accessed January 30, 2009).

PART II: SERVING YOUR EXTERNAL CUSTOMER

Chapter 8: Follow Apple's Five Steps of Service

1. Yukari Iwatani Kane and Ian Sherr, "Secrets from Apple's Genius Bar: Full Loyalty, No Negativity," *The Wall Street Journal*, June 15, 2011, http://

online.wsj.com/article/SB10001424052702304563104576364071955678908
.html (accessed December 31, 2011).

2. Jay Baer, "70% of Companies Ignore Customer Complaints on Twitter," Jay Baer's Convince & Convert, http://www.convinceandconvert.com/ social-media-monitoring/70-of-companies-ignore-customer-complaints-on-twitter/ (accessed December 31, 2011).

3. Carmine Gallo, "The New AT&T Customer Service Experience," *Forbes*, October 5, 2011, http://www.forbes.com/sites/carminegallo/2011/10/05/ the-new-att-customer-service-experience/ (accessed December 31, 2011).

Chapter 9: Reset Your Customer's Internal Clock

1. Vanessa Gallo, "Play Offense, Not Defense When You Make a Customer Service Blunder," Customer Service Stinks, Gallo Communications, November, 11, 2010, http://gallocommunications.com/2010/11/11/play-offense-not-defense-when-you-make-a-customer-service-blunder/ (accessed December 31, 2011).

Chapter 10: Sell the Benefit

1. Patty Cook, Apple customer, in discussion with the author, December 14, 2011.

2. ifoAppleStore.com, "10th Apple Poster," http://www.ifoapplestore.com/ db/10th-anniversary-poster/ (accessed December 31, 2011).

3. Wikipedia, "Apple A5," http://en.wikipedia.org/wiki/Apple_A5#cite_note-3 (accessed December 31, 2011).

Chapter 11: Unleash Your Customer's Inner Genius

1. Carolyn DiPiero, Apple customer, in discussion with the author, November 3, 2011.

2. YouTube, "Sexy Dance Time!" http://www.youtube.com/ watch?v=VoyYYU6JUXY (accessed December 31, 2011).

3. YouTube, "Working in Apple Retail," http://www.youtube.com/watch?v =CMj6G6ZALSw&feature=related (accessed December 31, 2011).

4. Simply Hired, "Apple Customer Service Rep, at Home," Simply Hired job description, posted December 27, 2011, http://www.simplyhired.com/ job-id/f4fobndq33/apple-customer-jobs/ (accessed December 31, 2011).

5. Ron Johnson, "What I Learned Building the Apple Store," *Harvard Business Review*, November, 21, 2011, http://blogs.hbr.org/cs/2011/11/what_i_ learned_building_the_ap.html (accessed December 31, 2011).

Chapter 12: Create Wow Moments

1. Macintosh unveiling 1984; Jobs quote.

2. YouTube, "Apple Music Event 2001—The First Ever iPod Introduction," http://www.youtube.com/watch?v=kN0SVBCJqLs&feature =related (accessed January 30, 2009).

3. YouTube, "Macworld 2007—Steve Jobs Introduces iPhone—Part 1," http://www.youtube.com/watch?v=PZoPdBh8KUs&feature=related (accessed January 30, 2009).

4. YouTube, "iPhone 4S—Full Apple Keynote—Apple Special Event, October 2011 (Full)," http://www.youtube.com/watch?v=dhdmZ7iNZYo (accessed December 31, 2011).

5. Jim Nicholas, president, FRSTeam, in discussion with the author, October 5, 2011.

Chapter 13: Rehearse the Script

1. YouTube, "Apple iPad 2 Keynote, Special Event, 2nd March, 2011 by Steve Jobs [Full]-[HQ]" http://www.youtube.com/watch?v=o3M8w6x-HTU (accessed December 31, 2011).

2. Apple Press Release, "Apple Launches iPad 2," Apple Press Info, March 2, 2011, http://www.apple.com/pr/library/2011/03/02Apple-Launches-iPad-2.html (accessed December 31, 2011).

3. YouTube, "Apple-iPad 2-TV Ad—We Believe," http://www.youtube.com/watch?v=tyEpaPEbjzI&feature=results_main&playnext=1&list=PL1819FC4D7ACCA678 (accessed December 31, 2011).

4. YouTube, "iPhone 4S—Full Apple Keynote—Apple Special Event, October 2011 (Full)," http://www.youtube.com/watch?v=dhdmZ7iNZYo (accessed December 31, 2011).

Chapter 14: Deliver a Consistent Experience

1. YouTube, "An Emotional Tribute to Steve Jobs at Ginza Apple Store in Tokyo Japan (ID-1133)," http://www.youtube.com/watch?v=tmIHOcR97WI (accessed December 31, 2011).

2. Ron Johnson, "What I Learned Building the Apple Store," *Harvard Business Review*, November, 21, 2011, http://blogs.hbr.org/cs/2011/11/what_i_learned_building_the_ap.html (accessed December 31, 2011).

3. American Express, "2011 Global Customer Service Barometer: Market Comparison of Findings," A research report prepared for American Express, http://about.americanexpress.com/news/docs/2011x/AXP_2011_csbar_market.pdf (accessed December 31, 2011).

4. Yukari Iwatani Kane and Ian Sherr, "Secrets from Apple's Genius Bar: Full Loyalty, No Negativity," *The Wall Street Journal*, June 15, 2011, http://online.wsj.com/article/SB10001424052702304563104576364071955678908.html (accessed December 31, 2011).

5. Lior Arussy, "Exceptional Service: Customer Experience, Self-Service and the Human Interaction," Strativity Group, Inc., 2009, http://ct6.pagepointhosting.com/files2/exceptional_service.pdf (accessed December 31, 2011).

6. Carmine Gallo, "Lush: Happy People Selling Happy Soap," *Business Management Daily*, August 16, 2011, http://www.businessmanagementdaily.com/13908/lush-happy-people-selling-happy-soap (accessed December 31, 2011).

7. http://www.forbes.com/sites/carminegallo/2011/11/11/01/business-renegade-zappos-tony-hsieh/

PART III: SETTING THE STAGE

Chapter 15: Eliminate the Clutter

1. Jim Dalrymple and Peter Cohen, "Jonathan Ive Gives Some Insight into His Designs," The Loop, June 11, 2009, http://www.loopinsight .com/2009/06/11/jonathan-ive-gives-some-insight-into-his-designs/ (accessed December 31, 2011).
2. George Beahm, editor, *I, Steve: Steve Jobs in His Own Words* (Chicago, IL: B2 Books, 2011), 93.
3. Cliff Edwards, "Commentary: Sorry, Steve: Here's Why Apple Stores Won't Work," *Bloomberg Businessweek*, May 21, 2001, http://www.businessweek. com/magazine/content/01_21/b3733059.htm (accessed December 31, 2011).
4. Ibid.
5. Ibid.
6. A. K. Pradeep, *The Buying Brain: Secrets for Selling to the Subconscious Mind* (NY: John Wiley & Sons, Inc., 2010), 58.
7. Ibid, 178.
8. Steve Kaufman, "Happy Birthday, Apple Stores," VMSD, July 1, 2011, http://vmsd.com/content/happy-birthday-apple-stores (accessed December 31, 2011).
9. Gary Allen, blogger, www.ifoAppleStore.com, in discussion with the author, October 11, 2011.
10. Carmine Gallo, "Copying Kinko's Success," *Bloomberg Businessweek*, July 11, 2008, http://www.businessweek.com/smallbiz/content/jul2008/ sb20080711_375397.htm (accessed December 31, 2011).
11. Vanessa Gallo, "Bad Breath, Dirty Toilets, and Other Ways to Piss Away Your Customers," Customer Service Stinks, Gallo Communications, June 21, 2009, http://gallocommunications.com/2009/06/21/bad-breath-dirty -toilets-and-other-ways-to-piss-away-your-customers/ (accessed December 31, 2011).

Chapter 16: Pay Attention to Design Details

1. Walter Isaacson, *Steve Jobs* (NY: Simon & Schuster, 2011), 78.
2. Ibid., 129.
3. Ibid, 134.
4. Ibid, 133.
5. Ibid, 126.
6. Steve Jobs for Fortune, "Apple's One-Dollar-a-Year Man," *Fortune*, January 24, 2000, CNNMoney.com, http://money.cnn.com/magazines/ fortune/fortune_archive/2000/01/24/272277/ (accessed December 31, 2011).
7. http://www.forbes.com/sites/velocity/2011/10/05/yves-behar-steve-jobs- changed-my-life
8. ifoAppleStore.com, "10th Apple Poster," http://www.ifoapplestore.com/ db/10th-anniversary-poster/ (accessed December 31, 2011).

9. Starbucks Gossip, "Starbucks Chairman Warns of 'The Commoditization of the Starbucks Experience,'" Starbucks Gossip, February 23, 2007, http://starbucksgossip.typepad.com/_/2007/02/starbucks_chair_2.html (accessed December 31, 2011).

10. Howard Schultz with Joanne Gordon, *Onward: How Starbucks Fought for Its Life Without Losing the Soul* (NY: Rodale, 2011), 274.

11. J. C. Ho, co-owner, Funnel Mill, in discussion with the author, December 22, 2011.

12. Ibid.

Chapter 17: Design Multisensory Experience

1. YouTube, "Apple—Steve Jobs Introduces the First Apple Store Retail 2001," YouTube, http://www.youtube.com/watch?v=OJtQeMHGrgc (accessed December 31, 2011).

2. ifoAppleStore.com, "10th Apple Poster," http://www.ifoapplestore.com/db/10th-anniversary-poster/ (accessed December 31, 2011).

3. IfoAppleStore.com, "The Stores," http://www.ifoapplestore.com/the_stores.html (accessed December 31, 2011).

4. Ron Johnson, "What I Learned Building the Apple Store," *Harvard Business Review*, November, 21, 2011, http://blogs.hbr.org/cs/2011/11/what_i_learned_building_the_ap.html (accessed December 31, 2011).

5. A. K. Pradeep, *The Buying Brain: Secrets for Selling to the Subconscious Mind* (NY: John Wiley & Sons, Inc., 2010), 177.

6. Ibid., 176.

7. Johnson, op.cit.

8. James Fielding quote, "Disney Rebooting Its Retail Stores...La Apple," December 10, 2011, http://www.menafn.com/qn_news_story.asp?storyid=%7Badcb4953-cada-47e8-808e-2d3b368a0738%7D (accessed January 22, 2012).

Conclusion: The Soul of Apple

1. YouTube, "Apple iPad 2 Keynote, Special Event, March 2011," http://www.youtube.com/watch?v=TGxEQhdi1AQ (accessed December 31, 2011).

2. Thomas Friedman and Michael Mandelbaum, *That Used to Be Us: How America Fell Behind in the World It Invented and How We Can Come Back* (NY: Farrar, Straus and Giroux, 2011), 78.

3. Ibid., 133.

4. Charlie Rose, "John Lasseter, Director and the Chief Creative Officer at Pixar and Walt Disney Animation Studios," with John Lasseter in *Movies, TV & Theater*, December 2, 2011, http://www.charlierose.com/view/interview/12024 (accessed December 31, 2011).

Index

CARMINE GALLO is the communications coach for the world's most admired global brands. A former anchor and correspondent for CNN and CBS, Gallo has addressed executives at Intel, Cisco, Google, Coca-Cola, Pfizer, and many others. Gallo writes "My Communications Coach," a regular column for Forbes.com. He has written several internationally bestselling and award-winning books, including *The Innovation Secrets of Steve Jobs, The Presentation Secrets of Steve Jobs,* and *The Power of foursquare.* Gallo has been featured in the *Wall Street Journal,* the *New York Times, Success Magazine,* and on CNBC. He lives in Pleasanton, California, with his wife and two daughters.

Carmine Gallo can be contacted at www.carminegallo.com.

Inside: The Ten Secrets to dynamic and memorable presentations

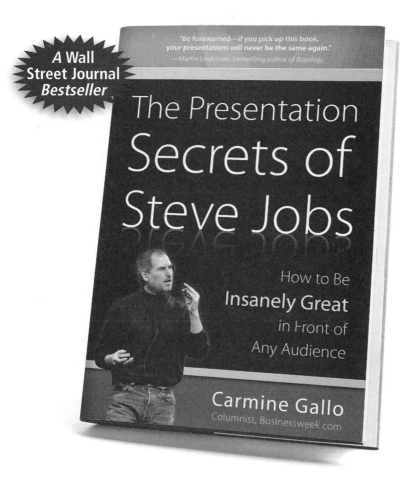

A Wall Street Journal Bestseller

"Be forewarned—if you pick up this book, your presentations will never be the same again."
—Martin Lindstrom, bestselling author of *Buyology*

The Presentation Secrets of Steve Jobs

How to Be **Insanely Great** in Front of Any Audience

Carmine Gallo
Columnist, Businessweek.com

"*... Like no other book* The Presentation Secrets of Steve Jobs *captures the formula Steve used to enthrall audiences*"
—Rob Enderle, The Enderle Group

Discover the Seven Principles
behind every breakthrough ide[a]

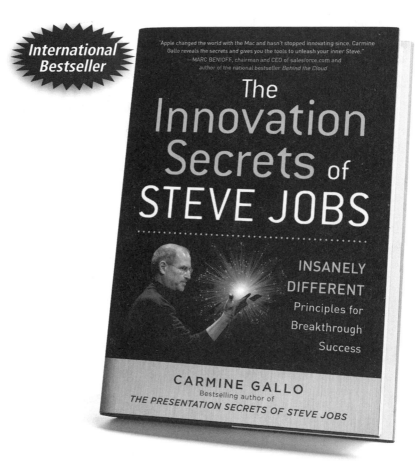

International Bestseller

"Apple changed the world with the Mac and hasn't stopped innovating since. Carmine Gallo reveals the secrets and gives you the tools to unleash your inner Steve."
—MARC BENIOFF, chairman and CEO of salesforce.com and author of the national bestseller *Behind the Cloud*

The
Innovation
Secrets of
STEVE JOBS

INSANELY DIFFERENT
Principles for Breakthrough Success

CARMINE GALLO
Bestselling author of
THE PRESENTATION SECRETS OF STEVE JOBS

"An inspiring roadmap for anyone who wants to live a life of passion and purpose.
—Tony Hsieh, *author of* Delivering Happiness an[d] CEO of Zappos.com, In[c.]